FIRST UNITED METHODIST
CHURCH LIBRARY
Huron, S. D.

DISCARD

The Scandal and the Star

D1528404

The Scandal and the Star

by W. Robert McClelland

CBP Press

St. Louis, Missouri

© 1988 CBP Press
All rights reserved. No part of this book may be reproduced without the publisher's written permission. Address: CBP Press, Box 179, St. Louis, MO 63166.

Unless otherwise indicated, all scripture quotations are from the Revised Standard Version of the Bible, copyrighted 1946, 1952, © 1971, 1973, by the Division of Christian Education of the National Council of Churches of Christ in the United States of America.

Library of Congress Cataloging-in-Publication Data
McClelland, W. Robert (William Robert), 1931-
    The scandal and the star / by W. Robert McClelland.
        p.   cm.
    ISBN 0-8272-3430-9 : $8.95
    1. Jesus Christ—Nativity. 2. Jesus Christ—Person and offices.
3. Christian life—1960- I. Title.
BT315.2.M34 1988
232.9'21—dc19   88-9507
                                                CIP

Printed in the United States of America

Contents

Lo, [children] are a heritage from the LORD,
        the fruit of the womb a reward.
Like arrows in the hand of a warrior
        are the [children] of one's youth.
Happy is the man who has
        his quiver full of them! (Psalm 127:3-5)

This book is dedicated to my children, whose advent into life has brought incarnations of divine delight.
- Steven Robert, my beloved son, in whom I am well pleased.
- Christie Ann, a gift of grace, whose own birth story is itself a miracle narrative.
- Susan Dorrine, who came dancing with a joyful little song in her head and at last gets the acknowledgment so long requested.

- . . . also their two sisters, whom they never had the privilege of knowing but who were, in their own way, reminders of God's goodness.

Preface

The intent of this little volume is to free the birth of Jesus from sentimental and seasonal stereotypes. But if we are to consider his nativity and its significance with any serious intent, we must open the Bible and read the only accounts that we have of the originating event, seeing them *as if for the first time*.

To begin, let us imagine a public opinion poll taken among the angelic host of heaven. The questionnaire asks: What should typify the Most High's grand entrance onto the stage of history? How should God come among the human race? The choices are:

(a) With glory, coming on the clouds of heaven with trumpet fanfare and the Mormon Tabernacle Choir singing "The Hallelujah Chorus" in the background.

(b) With power, gathering a mighty army that will bear arms and crush all opposition to the divine will.

(c) As a Wonder Worker, focusing on the needs of the people, filling their stomachs and healing their diseases.

(d) None of the above.

Imagine the consternation among the angelic host as they consider the possibilities and then discover, much to their amazement, that God has decided on answer (d): "None of the above." God will not come in glory. The Most High will sire a son who will be born in a stable. The manure will have to be cleared away to make room for him. He will not come in power. The Holy One will be born as a helpless babe who can only nurse at his mother's breast. And when the child grows into adulthood, he will not secure an agent to book him as a wonder worker concerned with the entertainment or needs of the public. By midlife, he will have turned his back on the vocations of teaching and healing to pick up a cross and die as a common criminal. Thus, God affirms the last option as the correct choice.

What is yet more amazing is the realization that the Bible seems to understand God's preference for this last option as typical. It tells story after story in which this formula can apply.

Consider, for example, the Old Testament story of Abraham. God comes to Abraham with an offer: I will be your God and you and your descendants after you will be my people; I will make of you a nation more numerous than all the sands of all the seashores. God makes the promise, mind you, to a man and woman who are well along in years and for whom the period of childbearing has long ago ceased to be. The Bible storytellers leave us with the question: How will God do this? How will the Promise Maker be a Promise Keeper and bring forth nations from an old, old man and a barren woman?

    (a) They will adopt a child.
    (b) They will have children by Abraham's slave, Hagar.
    (c) God will have to choose someone else.
    (d) None of the above.

The Bible indicates the last choice is the correct one. God "has a better idea." God will bring forth a son, a legitimate heir, from the barren womb of Sarah. The Holy One will make the life springs rise again in the old, old man, Abraham. God's choice is "None of the above."

Or turn to the account of the Exodus, a story about an enslaved people who are held in bondage by the oppressive economic system of the Egyptians. The question that the writers must face is: How are we to understand our Covenant Partner?

    (a) As a God who advocates law and order and believes that differences should be negotiated, taken to the courts, and settled through the legal channels provided for handling disputes.
    (b) As a God who rewards hard work and frowns upon laziness, assuring those who want to get ahead that they can climb the ladder of success by exerting themselves and applying themselves diligently to their work.

(c) As a God of peace, who calls us to be content with our lot in life and bids us fit the yoke of spiritual discipline to our necks in order to learn the hard lessons of patience and humility.

(d) None of the above.

The Bible again makes it clear that (d) is the correct answer. God is not to be understood in any of the above categories. The Lion of Judah is a God who champions the cause of the underdog and will fight on their behalf. Far from being impartial, Yahweh is an advocate for their cause even espousing violence and bloodshed.

Luke tells the story of Zacchaeus, a despised tax collector, who made his living by cheating everyone. When Jesus came to town Zacchaeus, being very short of stature, decided to climb a tree for a better look. Jesus noticed him out on his limb, but the question was: What should he as Messiah do? "Try to change Zacchaeus?," the townspeople would have scoffed, "You might as well try to turn stones into bread!" Those things just do not happen. The options, therefore, were quite clear:

(a) Scold Zacchaeus for being a sinner.

(b) Ignore Zacchaeus because to recognize him in any way gives tacit support to his dishonest dealings.

(c) Laugh at Zacchaeus. He is, after all, a ridiculous spectacle: up a tree.

But Jesus said: "You've forgotten the option again: (d) None of the above." He asks Zacchaeus to come down from the tree and invites himself to Zacchaeus' house for dinner and conversation. And the next day the story is flying around town: Zacchaeus is a changed man. He's not only giving back what he's stolen, but he's giving it back four times over!

Often Bible stories are read in the same way that we read children's fairy tales: "Once upon a time . . . and they all lived happily ever after." And frequently the nativity stories suffer the same seasonal fate as, " 'Twas the night before Christmas and all through the house. . . . "

But to re-examine these stories in light of the familiar and obvious options (a), (b), (c), and then to discover the writer's preference for (d) None of the above, is to see that these stories

9

display a radically creative approach to life. They are more illustrative of a view of life than of miraculous happenings. They are stories that refuse to accept the established categories of life as fixed. A response to life that says, "None of the above," is a response that sees that the options offered do not fit. That is why Jesus insisted, "My kingdom is not of this world." Unfortunately, we have assumed that he was talking about heaven. But to look at the stories, and especially the nativity narratives, from a kingdom point of view is to discover an imaginative approach to *this* life. The categories of this world are not finally settled. The definitions that fetter us are not forged in steel. Jesus and the Gospel writers look at life from a different perspective, and therein lies the kingdom of God. They invite us to live by faith in a God who consistently offers another option than those seen by the authorities and power brokers of this world—an option that fits "None of the above."

Are these stories and the way they are told important to us and the way we view our lives? You, of course, will have to answer that for yourself. But an architect once told me, "If you build a house, you will want to spend plenty of time designing it. You want to be sure that it's the kind of home you want to live in, because once it is built, the home will design you."

It will be clear, I trust, that I have taken the stories of Jesus' birth seriously, if not literally. I hope these pages will cause you to think about them again, about how they have been told and how you want to tell them. Once we tell the story, once we have given it shape, it will shape us. The story of Jesus' birth can be seen, not as a romantic myth of merely seasonal interest, but as a story that determines our destiny. Across all of the traditional, orthodox, and "correct" answers to life, all of the assumptions and definitions that shape who we are and determine our future— across all of these, the story of Christ's coming writes "None of the above" and offers instead the possibilities of the Kingdom.

In any endeavor of this sort, acknowledgments are always in order. To those who have read the manuscript, making corrections and offering suggestions—Bonnie Montle, William Gay, and Herb Lambert—I offer heartfelt thanks until they are better paid. And as always, I remain indebted to you, dear reader, for doing me the honor of reading my work.

W. Robert McClelland

1

Born in a Barn

Poor manners are sometimes greeted with the sarcastic taunt, "Were you born in a barn?" Well, Jesus was! And therein lies the tale of this book. Make no mistake. The birth of Jesus was an embarrassment to early Christians and when freed from its seasonal sentimentality, creates for modern believers a real crisis of faith. Open the New Testament and the scandal hits you squarely between the eyes.

There in Matthew's Christmas story is Mary, the pregnant girl without a husband. There, too, is Joseph, on the verge of canceling the wedding. The townspeople, no doubt, were buzzing about Mary, the girl who "had to get married."

Luke's birth narrative is just as embarrassing. He makes it plain that the locus of divine disclosure was not on top of some Mount Olympus, high above human corruption, but in a filthy, smelly, manure-ridden barn. Christmas cards tend to gloss over Luke's offensiveness by romanticizing the picture. Fat little cherub angels flutter around the participants, all of whom are sporting halos, and all of which is intended to reassure us that it really was not as bad as Luke portrays it.

The later life of Jesus is no less scandalous. The stories told in the gospels, if taken at face value, picture Jesus as a person who dawdled away his time dreaming utopian dreams and talking with people on the hillsides around the Sea of Galilee instead of—as the diplomatic phrase puts it—finding gainful employment. By his mid-thirties he had acquired a police record, been excommunicated from his church, and died a disgrace to his family and friends. But, then, what else could you expect, the social workers might have said, from such a questionable beginning?

Nevertheless, when Christmas rolls around, the scandal does

not seem to bother us. It is seldom mentioned and certainly not as a subject of gossip. Is it because we are too embarrassed to speak of it? Perhaps. But more likely, it is because we do not even *see* the scandal.

> Now when Jesus was born in Bethlehem of Judea in the days of Herod the king, behold, wise men from the East came to Jerusalem, saying, ''Where is he who has been born king of the Jews? For we have seen his star in the East, and have come to worship him'' (Matthew 2:1,2).

If we too come to worship him, it is because the scandal is transformed by the light of that star—a star that lights up the landscape so that we see this baby conceived out of wedlock as God's appointment with humanity. We see the scene as clearly as the wee lad who, when asked by the Sunday school teacher to give his version of the Christmas story, came up with this literary effort in which we can see the innocent beauty of our own unquestioning faith.

> It was a snowie day.
> And it was sunday.
> The people were going to church,
> And they sang songs,
> and did what you usually do.
> All could not buleve ther eyes.
> And the doctor came and said
> that they were not seeing things.
> Cause ther was a babby ther
> and on his shirt it said JESUS.

''On his shirt it said JESUS.'' If only it were that obvious! If only a neon sign had flashed, ''Jesus, the Christ.'' If only his swaddling clothes had been lettered in big bold print, ''This is not a scandal. This is the Son of God!''

But it was not that obvious. Only a star indicated that this child was different from all of the other children born that night. It was a star, and only a star, that indicated this was not just another statistic, but rather the fulfillment of the divine promise. And if the Gospel writers had not been looking up to see the star, they probably would have dismissed the incident as another pathetic case for public aid. We would never have heard of Matthew and Luke, much less Mark and John, and certainly not Jesus. The joy of the occasion was clearly not obvious to Joseph. But for the generosity of Joseph, Jesus might have been called something other than the "Son of God." The whole episode is not without its humor, however. Picture obviously pregnant Mary coming home to Joseph with her arms filled with groceries.

"Honey, you'll never guess what happened to me today. You see, there was this angel. . . . "

"This what?" Joseph might say, staring at her in stunned disbelief.

"This angel," Mary would insist.

"Righhhhhhhhht!" says Joseph, looking skeptically over his glasses.

But the poor fellow had nothing more concrete to go on. Matthew makes it plain that Joseph had only a dream on which to hang his love. Only a dream to trust. Only a dream flying in the face of the brutal reality that Mary, his betrothed, was pregnant. It was a dream—and only a dream—that indicated this was not a scandal to be quietly hushed up, but the Messiah, come at last to his people.

Christians celebrate Christmas because a star lights these scandalous scenes as divine drama.

The problem for us sophisticated moderns is that we do not take the star seriously. If we talk about the Bethlehem star at all, it is to discuss its astronomy. Even biblical scholars frequently dismiss it as the fabrication of Matthew to fulfill an Old Testament prophecy regarding the coming of the Messianic age.

But the star is the crux of the matter, and the issue that it illumines for us is as contemporary as your life or mine, namely: *What do we do with the down-to-earth reality, the stuff of which our quite ordinary and frequently scandalous lives are made?*

What, for example, do we do with the girl who becomes pregnant before marriage? Especially if she is your girlfriend or my daughter? How do we face tomorrow, let alone our friends?

What do we do when we have been the cause of some irreparable harm that cannot be undone no matter how many tears of remorse are shed? You are the driver of a car, let us say, that strikes and kills a child. The youngster darted into the street in front of you. It was clearly not your fault. But can you say, "Oh, well, I'll get over it?" What *right* have you to get over it? How do you *dare* give yourself permission to live another day? No matter who is at fault, the child is still dead and you are responsible.

Or, if that is too extreme, what do we say when we hurt someone we love? To say, "I'm sorry. It won't happen again," is pitifully naive because it is only a matter of time until we hurt that person again in the same or some other way. It is human nature. How, then, do we *dare* to love again?

And yet we do! All of us do. But on what basis?

Albert Camus, the French philosopher, argued that the basic human question is whether or not to commit suicide. The only way we can make such a decision is to assume something about life. There is no unassailable proof that life is good, bad, or indifferent. The evidence is conflicting. Responding to the data by saying, "Yes, I will call life 'good' and choose to continue with it," is to make a radical affirmation about life. It is, if you will, an act of faith.

The fact is that we all live by faith. Faith is simply a name for the star that lights the raw data of reality with the rays of meaning and hope. To choose life rather than suicide is an assertion that living holds more promise than dying. But we have no proof of this. We can only assume that tomorrow will bring more fulfillment than doing ourselves in today. And that assumption is the star that lights the landscape of our otherwise quite ordinary, and sometimes discouraging, lives with promise and hope.

It is, then, the star that makes all the difference in how we view these nativity narratives. It transforms scandal into gospel. In the last analysis, all we can say about these gospel stories is that there was nothing to distinguish that babe in a barn from a hundred others who were born that night—except a star. A star that some wise men from the East *assumed* would point to the Messiah King.

For us, the star is of more interest than merely an astronomical curiosity. Its light not only offers us a perspective that transforms the ordinary scandal into a divine revelation, but it also represents the faith perspective by which every one of us lives.

Too often, faith has been understood as a set of beliefs about supernatural realities held by religious people. Consequently, many conclude that faith is just not their "thing" because they

14

do not hold such beliefs. They may conclude that they do not have, nor do they need, faith. Faith is, thereby, regarded as a *noun*, something that can be taken or left alone.

But when we look at faith as a *verb*, the picture changes, and we can see it as an inescapable fact of life. To live at all, is to live by faith. The two go together. Faith is living *as though*—as though this is true or that is to be expected. Faith is *living as though* life is hopeful or despairing, *as though* it is meaningful or absurd, *as though* God is present or absent, *as though* Christ is Lord or irrelevant.

Suppose, for example, that you happen to meet a stranger on a plane who engages you in a conversation. You can respond *as though* it is an invasion of your privacy, or *as though* it is an interesting opportunity filled with possibilities, *as though* it is something to be done dutifully in the name of polite civility, or *as though* it offers a chance to discover something of another person's mystery. We can look upon such a conversation as being mere coincidence or as having hidden meaning. We can choose to enter it as idle chatter or as having ultimate significance for reasons yet unknown to us. What we *assume* about the conversation either predisposes us to be open to the experience or closed to it, expectantly entering into it or enduring it with indifference or hostility.

Clearly, to function in the world with any sense of awareness we must make some assumptions about the meaning of the experiences that wash over us. My faith assumptions about life may be different from yours, but both of our lives are made meaningful by one set of faith assumptions or another. We literally bet our lives on them. Consequently, we need to make conscious use of our rational powers to examine these assumptions and be intentional about our selection of those by which we live. For if we do not make a conscious commitment of our lives to one set of faith assumptions, we will, nevertheless, back blindly into another set. The question is never: Shall I, or shall I not live by faith? The only question is: By which faith shall I live? This is why it behooves us to consider again these Christmas stories. *They invite us to make some remarkable assumptions about life, assumptions that may yield relief, freedom, and joy.*

Living by faith is a uniquely human experience. It is one of the characteristics that differentiate us from other forms of life.

15

Lower forms of animal life operate largely by instinct. They react to life around them. But we human animals have developed the ability to make value judgments about our existence. We make some assessment of our experiences. We can, therefore, choose to *act* on the basis of our assessments rather than merely *react* out of instinct.

One little boy inquired about the dust under his bed. "Is it true, Mommy," he asked, "that we are created from dust?" "Yes," his mother answered. He continued his investigation. "Is it true that when we die we return to dust?" "That's right," she replied. "Well then, Mommy, somebody is under the bed, but I don't know whether he's coming or going."

Many of us can identify with the quandary of not knowing whether we are coming or going, but it goes much deeper than the frenzied, harried feeling that comes over us when we are too busy. The depth of that feeling is shown by our questions about the meaning and purpose of life, or by the lump we feel in our throat when we contemplate our aging and death. It is not simply an attack of nostalgia that sweeps over us. It is, rather, the realization that we pass this way but once. Whether we verbalize it or not, the question that haunts us is: What are we to make of our existence between the dust of creation and the dust of the grave? That is a question we alone as human beings are privileged to ask, *and answer*. But the answer is an act of faith. We may come from dust, and we may return to dust, but between these what makes us human is the faith-act of living as though . . . something is true.

One clear benefit of faith (living as though . . .) for the human animal is that our assumptions about life provide us with a basis for rational and responsible action. We can make decisions that are consistent with our basic beliefs and that, thereby, enable us to be intentional about living. If we assume, let us say, that we will be dead next week, we will do some things today and leave other things undone. These actions will be quite different if we are planning a trip to Europe in a month.

Another benefit of faith is that it enables us to interpret life in some meaningful way. We gather our faith assumptions together in collections that serve as star-stories. They give us a perspective on life. Necessarily, we search for, and either find or create, some kind of meaningful interpretation of the raw data of our experience. It is essential to our mental health.

Not even God can escape the need to organize the primal chaos into some kind of story. "In the beginning was the Word . . . ," is the way John puts it (John 1:1). It was a Word through which, and by which, all things were created and organized. As with God, so with us. We need an organizing word or story that unifies the whole and provides a purposeful perspective by which to live.

But while living by a faith story is inevitable and useful—indeed, crucial—it is also risky. The very nature of living as though . . . is that we live by assumptions that cannot be proved. We walk by faith, not by sight. It is the nature of faith that it cannot be proved in advance. We cannot prove that tomorrow will ever dawn for us. We assume that it will and plan our activities accordingly. But we cannot prove today that tomorrow will come, nor that we will be here to enjoy it if it does. We assume it. The atheist is quick to point out that belief in God is an assumption for which there is no proof. What the atheist does not usually realize is that to say, "There is no God," is equally unprovable and just as much of a faith assumption.

Nevertheless, though faith assumptions cannot be proved in advance, they yield data that can be evaluated. In this respect, living by a faith story is similar to testing a hypothesis in the laboratory. The scientist must live as though the hypothesis is true until the experiment is concluded. Not until then will the scientist be able to evaluate the data and determine if the original hypothesis was valid, or needs modification. Similarly, unproven faith assumptions yield data as they are life-tested in the laboratory of our experience—data that can then be evaluated with respect to their value or validity.

As we might expect, the results of living by various faith assumptions differ widely. Faith stories that do not take into account *all* of reality—the scandalous as well as the sacred, suffering and death as well as health and life—are inadequate. They will sooner or later leave their holders hopelessly out of touch with reality, if not cynical and disillusioned. Thinking positively may offer temporary relief from the pain of minor headaches, but unless our world view does business with the negative realities of life, we are doomed to disappointment and disillusionment, if not extinction.

Seen in this light, Jesus' parable of house building is illuminating (Matthew 7:24-27). I gather from it that examining our faith stories and the living assumptions they embody is not just an academic exercise, but one of utmost pragmatic importance. If we are to get the most out of life, we need to build on solid rock; that is, we need to live by faith assumptions that take life readily into account, make sense of it, offer us a ground for hope, and provide motivation for responsible action. That may be the most important reason for giving serious consideration to the Jesus stories—not because they save souls or have to do with things supernatural, but because they take our scandalous humanity seriously and enable us to live joyously with it. Christian faith does not provide us with a view of heaven but a pair of spectacles through which we can view the barns that dot the landscape of our lives. It has to do with understanding life here and now, not merely some future life in the hereafter.

There is, then, nothing particularly spiritual about Christian faith. It is, in fact, quite worldly, since it has to do with scandals and barns. The believer is no more religious than the atheist. Both live by faith assumptions concerning the stuff of this quite ordinary life. To this extent, both are religious.

But the light of the Bethlehem star sheds a particular light on our situation. It offers those who have eyes to see that much needed ingredient for living: a sense of worth. Sometimes there seems precious little reason to value our lives and the permission to do so lies beyond the immediate situation. Often it lies only in the story we tell ourselves.

In his last message to his fiancée, written from a Nazi prison cell at Christmastime, 1944, Dietrich Bonhoeffer wrote, "What is happiness? It depends so little on the circumstances; it depends really only on that which happens inside a person. . . . "

Bonhoeffer's life and writing testify to a joy in his last days that depended little on the actual circumstances of his life and much on his assumptions about their meaning. Bonhoeffer, a Christian martyr, lived with the light of that Bethlehem star shining over the dark and dreary landscape of his jail cell. As a result, he saw his prison as a parish to be served. His confinement was viewed as purposeful rather than a tragic waste of time. He spent those days of confinement thinking and writing about the meaning of faith and ethical responsibility for Christians in a world "come of age.'' The letters and papers that he managed to smuggle out to his friend Eberhard Bethge before his execution have been a boon to contemporary theological discussion. Except for a story with a star, Bonhoeffer might have languished in his cell and succumbed to self-pity.

So we live by the stories we tell ourselves and come to believe as true. They shape our lives. The nativity narratives of Jesus claim in their awesomely simple way that we have been *accepted* by God. All good religions tell us something about God and urge us to lead a moral life. But the star stories dare to state that the Divine Word really became flesh and dwelt among us. The Holy One takes our scandalous humanity seriously to the point of identifying irrevocably with it. In the person of Jesus, our reach and God's grasp are one.

But these stories also invite our response—for or against, *pro* or *con*. For those of us who choose to believe (that is, to live as though . . .) these stories reveal divine truth. They will become our source of wisdom. Our understanding of God and ourselves, our view of life and its meaning, our values and our clues to responsible behavior will ultimately derive from the accounts of what happened in the stable of an obscure inn.

Nevertheless, it is a decision of the will to believe more than it is an emotional response of the heart or a reasoned conclusion of the mind. It is impossible to argue persons into believing the Christmas message and dishonest to manipulate them with theatrics. They either see it or they do not. The story of this babe born in a barn is like the burning blaze of a winter sunset. We are either amazed by its beauty, or it leaves us cold. We stand before the Christ story even as we stand before our own living and dying, and see it—if we see anything at all—as divine drama *because* it is seen by the light of the star, or we simply see an absurd scandal. We will either bet our lives on the view of life disclosed in the Christ story, or we will remain indifferent and choose, instead, some other faith perspective. Christian faith rests its case, not on logical proof or emotional hype, but on a risk to live as though. . . . We are quite literally gambling with our lives.

That is why, with reverent imagination and humble minds, we must look back to that first Christmas again and again, year after year, and see it as though for the first time; see it through the eyes of the Gospel writers. To those who have eyes to see and ears to hear, the good news of Christ's coming is the joyous affirmation that God speaks to peasants as well as priests, has taken up residence in barns as well as cathedrals, and cares for the illegitimate as well as the legitimate. In a baby born in a barn we read a remarkable story in which we discover, much to our amazement, that indeed our scandalous world is the place to look for the divine and not, as we have been led to believe, in the hallowed halls of holiness and perfection.

2

The Crisis of Christ

Now the birth of Jesus Christ took place in this way. When his mother Mary had been betrothed to Joseph, before they came together she was found to be with child of the Holy Spirit; and her husband Joseph, being a just man and unwilling to put her to shame, resolved to divorce her quietly. But as he considered this, behold, an angel of the Lord appeared to him in a dream, saying, "Joseph, son of David, do not fear to take Mary your wife, for that which is conceived in her is of the Holy Spirit; she will bear a son, and you shall call his name Jesus, for he will save his people from their sins." . . . When Joseph woke from sleep, he did as the angel of the Lord commanded him; he took his wife, but knew her not until she had borne a son; and he called his name Jesus (Matthew 1:18-21, 24-25).

This Jesus was a problem! Even before he was born he was a problem. He provided Joseph with, if not an immense headache, at least a massive identity crisis.

Frequently, the forces that drive a person into an identity crisis are mobilized by some disruptive trauma. It may be the loss of a job, the death of a loved one, a move to a new location, the breakup of a marriage, or the graying of hair. It may be a major occurrence or an insignificant event. For Joseph, it was the discovery that his fiancée was pregnant.

It is interesting how the various writers handle the incarnation. John treats the event philosophically, while Mark passes over it entirely. Luke is concerned with Mary, while Matthew is fascinated by Joseph. Their differences will be instructive. For now, however, let us note simply that in Christian tradition Mary is the one who gets the play, especially at Christmastime. All of the attention is on the lovely young Madonna, dressed in blue and holding the bambino. Joseph, if we think of him at all, stands in the background. We imagine him as middle-aged, rather colorless and conservative, but steady and dependable. Above all, sensible and rational.

For Mary, the conception of Jesus was a matter of unusual concern. But it is also clear from Luke's account that trusting came easily for Mary. After an initial period of some uneasiness, she accepted the fact without great questioning and was able to say to the angel, "Behold, I am the handmaid of the Lord; let it be to me according to your word" (Luke 1:38).

For Joseph, however, the conception of Jesus was a major trauma. It nearly blew the poor fellow out of the water! Joseph discovered, long before Sam Keen did, that the Holy Spirit is a wild dove, not a tame pigeon. For steady and dependable Joseph, steeped in conventional morality and knowledgeable in religious law, Mary's pregnancy was a fracturing experience. It totally destroyed his world. It was obvious to Joseph that Mary, his betrothed, was pregnant. It was equally clear, to him at least, that he was not the father of the child. The conclusion was inescapable: Mary had been "fooling around." By any moral or religious standard, such behavior was inexcusable. But Joseph was a rational man. He did not respond to the situation as an emotional adolescent. He did not buy a gun and shoot her. No, he did the sane thing and acted in a mature manner. He decided to put her away quietly, call the wedding off, and return the presents. No explanations. After all, maturity has its own kind of wisdom, and that would be a just and moral way to handle the whole sordid affair.

Joseph is to be commended. After all, Mary's account of it all comes up lame. Imagine, if you will, a high-school girl announcing to her peers, "I am pregnant, and it is by the Holy Spirit." Her announcement would be greeted, if not with laughter, at least with total disbelief. No one would buy her story. So Joseph's conclusion is understandable and his intention laudable.

Nevertheless, in the middle of his identity crisis, Joseph has a change of mind. He sees things differently. Similar to a conversion experience, what to him seemed so obvious is now not clear at all, and what was unthinkable becomes imperative. Joseph takes Mary as his wife—pregnancy and all. Matthew invites us to see in these scandalous events—these fracturing, disruptive, embarrassing events—that God was calling Joseph to trust the divine madness rather than his own conventional wisdom. I mean Trust with a capital "T." I am talking about Trust, which means an entire change of perspective.

Can you imagine what Joseph's cronies must have thought about his change of plans? All of them God-fearing, church-attending, Bible-reading, and law-abiding champions of God, motherhood, and country. They could only shake their heads at Joseph and whisper behind his back. "How Joseph has changed! We were all sympathetic and supportive when he would have nothing to with the woman. But now, look at him! He's actually embracing her and endorsing her behavior. He's even buying her story: her pregnancy an act of God. He's lost it, I fear."

Trust for Mary was as natural as breathing. But trust for Joseph was the death of a world view and the birth of a whole new way of looking at life. It required scrapping all of his old assumptions about life and God and going back to the drawing board.

When we first meet Joseph in the story he appears in the role of "Father Knows Best." The great American Dad—the epitome of cool control, sane, rational, unemotional, and on top of the situation. Our educational system trains us, and our culture demands that we learn how to raise questions, analyze problems, and find solutions. We are encouraged to set goals, and success is measured by our ability to achieve them. In a technological society, we must manipulate our environment and control the variables. We have a culturally conditioned need to be in charge of our lives and destinies. Sam Keen speaks of this neurotic need to be in control as the great American sin.

> One symptom of the American way of sin, we're told, is that a third to one-half of Americans suffer from constipation and hemorrhoids. We are also told that salvation from this sin is Preparation H. It is typical of the American character that we believe in scientific nostrums. In reality, constipation and hemorrhoids are philosophical problems that science and medicine cannot solve. From childhood we are told that we must control ourselves. The head must

23

control the body. The body must function regularly and follow orders. It must eliminate waste every twelve hours. To comply with our constipated need for control and order, to do our duty regularly, we push our bodies. We push until the pushing is translated into hemorrhoids. This is the model of unfaith, of untrust. Hemorrhoids, the national disease, is the sign of our paranoia or, in theological terms, of our untrust.[1]

Joseph, like so many of us, was constipated: physically, emotionally, spiritually. Nothing could be admitted into his frame of reference that did not fit, or over which he had no control. Then God entered the scene. In these scandalous events God was nudging Joseph to let go of his wisdom and trust the divine foolishness, to let go of his morality and trust a dream that came to him in the middle of the night. In these painful and unplanned events, the Holy One was inviting Joseph to trust the divine madness that cut him loose from all the conventional anchors that gave his life stability and security—anchors that also weighed him down and held him back. Joseph was to discover that authentic life involves being broken open and remaining porous to the scandalous intrusions of Reality. To trust God meant accepting the intrusion of Mary's pregnancy as a gift of divine grace. It meant embracing the child to be born as the Son of God.

By so doing, he makes his problem ours.

One of the Christmas carols invites us to ask the question "What Child Is This?" Good question! And it enlarges the circle of crisis as rings expand from a stone thrown into the pond. The ripples now become a tidal wave threatening to engulf us.

Rudolph Otto, in describing the confrontation with God, speaks of the Holy breaking into and destroying our human categories for understanding the divine encounter and shattering the nice neat coherences that we have managed to make. To encounter the Holy One is to have our common sense, our standard-brand morality, our accustomed rationality blown to the wind.

What child *is* this who was conceived out of wedlock? What child *is* this who was born with the hint of scandal about him and lived out his life with the question of legitimacy hanging over him?

If this is just another welfare case, just another pathetic statistic—even though the child grew up to become a great and exemplary figure—then the question dissolves, along with any reason for celebrating Christmas. We can simply note in passing that Jesus, like Abraham Lincoln, was born of humble parents, rose from obscurity to prominence, and attracted a following. In short, he made something of himself. Good show! Perhaps his birthday is worth remembering, but hardly celebrating with such excitement, and certainly not worth the long consideration that the four weeks of Advent demand of believers each year. The point is, if we are to celebrate Advent and Christmas, we must do so by the light that the Gospels shed on the matter. Otherwise, it is much ado about nothing.

So, the question: "What child is this?"

Matthew says, "All this took place to fulfil what the Lord had spoken by the prophet: 'Behold, a virgin shall conceive and bear a son, and his name shall be called Emmanuel,' (which means, God with us)" (Matthew 1:22-23). This child is God with us. He cites an Old Testament prophecy in Isaiah which claims that the Messiah's name shall be called, "Emmanuel," that is, God with us, and therein lies our problem. What does it mean to say this child is God with us? Put another way: How is our understanding of God altered when we look at the birth of this baby born in a barn?

Whatever else it may mean, it clearly disrupts all of the traditional categories for understanding the Holy One. And because they are traditional, any change in them creates a crisis of faith for us.

Take, for example, the traditional category of God's *omnipotence*.

Generally, we think of God in superlatives—the highest, the biggest, the best. We easily speak of the Holy One as almighty, all-knowing, and ever-present.

But Matthew's star invites us to see the Holy One bathed, not in the light of divine superlatives, but in those of radically human categories. Matthew invites us to think of God in terms of ourselves. His star shows us the dimension of the divine inscribed within our very humanity. With all of its bumps and warts, our image is used to convey the character of God. When someone commented to Mark Twain that Man was created in the image of God, he quipped, "Yes, and Man, being a gentleman, returned the favor and created God in his.'' There is profound truth in Twain's observation, as Matthew understood long ago.

Karl Barth warned about the dangers in speaking of God by talking about humanity with a loud voice. But an even greater danger lies in making the Holy One so remote that we successfully remove God from life in the world. One of the ways by which we isolate God is in emphasizing God's perfection. When we think of God in terms of superlatives, that is, all-powerful, all-wise, all-knowing; we create a god who is perfect. And since the world in which we live is made up of the quite ordinary, mundane, and even scandalous—in short, since there is no such thing as perfection in *this* world—we effectively insulate heavenly visions from earthly concerns.

What is at stake here is not purity of doctrine, but relationship with God. Matthew is a storyteller, not a theologian. Rather than iron out all of the inconsistencies in the name of pure doctrine, he passes over them and portrays instead a God with whom we can identify. The star reveals the true identity of Jesus. He is Emmanuel, that is, God with us. The Bible invites us to assume that God is more like us than different from us. Rather than drawing on the vocabulary of superlatives to speak of the Holy One—all of which may be theologically correct—we are given permission to think of God in the radically human categories that characterize our irrational and often scandalous lives.

Matthew, in this case, stands in the most orthodox of traditions. Inscribed on the very first page of our Bibles is a statement which, if assumed to be true, leads us to think that the best way of knowing God is to look in a mirror. We are created in the image of God (Genesis 1:26). At the very least that seems to suggest that knowing ourselves gives us our best clue for understanding God.

Nevertheless, it has always been easy and tempting for Christians to assume that God is all-powerful and has the power to do whatever God wants. "There is nothing God cannot do," we frequently declare. Such an understanding of the Supreme Being has been embodied in the church's creeds from the very beginning. The familiar Apostles' Creed, for instance, speaks of God as "Almighty, Maker of heaven and earth." The belief that the Almighty God is in control not only serves as the foundation of traditional Christian thinking but is well received in a society that is obviously in love with body-building and impressed by big bucks, at a time in history when horsepower and megaton might seem to direct the course of human events. The Holy One, therefore, steals into our midst almost unnoticed through Matthew's story of a mother and a helpless baby to be called Emmanuel—God with us.

The silliness slaps us full in the face. An omnipotent God with us? Ludicrous! Yet there it is. The story invites us to look for God's presence, not in places of strength and authority, but in the locale of human weakness and scandal. The very thought strikes us at first as rank heresy if not outright blasphemy. Our initial response is to ask what can a baby do? Clearly, not much. This one, at least, is quite helpless, dependent on his mother to nourish him and utterly defenseless—a totally vulnerable God.

In the take charge attitude of our high-tech world, we assume the variables can be controlled and must be manipulated. Because of the emerging capabilities of genetic engineering, we increasingly assume life itself will yield to our desires. A god-figure born in a barn as a helpless babe is irrelevant at the point where we live our lives. Our gods must be at least as capable as we in getting things done. Gentleness is not a macho virtue, and weakness is downright disgusting. Results are what count. Patience and humility may be acceptable for peasants but not for potentates. Self-respecting gods are sovereign and sit enthroned in heavenly places, where they rule in holy isolation over the affairs of the cosmos. The creation jumps to their commands. They get things done!

Jewish theologian Richard Rubenstein contends that after Auschwitz it is impossible for Jews to believe in God in any traditional sense. He argues that either the Almighty is dead or, worse, demonic. If we begin with the assumption that omnipotence must be a characteristic of the Holy One, then such a conclusion must inevitably follow.

Although the incident is trivial in comparison to the Holocaust, Huckleberry Finn comes to a similar conclusion when his prayers go unanswered:

Miss Watson she took me in the closet and prayed, but nothing come of it. She told me to pray every day, and whatever I asked for I would get it. But it warn't so; I tried it. Once I got a fish-line, but no hooks. It warn't any good to me without hooks. I tried for the hooks three or four times, but somehow I couldn't make it work. By and by, one day, I asked Miss Watson to try for me, but she said I was a fool; she never told me why, and I couldn't make it out no way.

I set down, one time, back in the woods, and had a long think about it. I says to myself, if a body can get anything they pray for, why don't Deacon Winn get back the money he lost on pork? Why can't the widow get back her silver snuff-box that was stole? Why can't Miss Watson fat up? No, says I to myself, there ain't nothing in it.[2]

We may smile at the naiveté of Huckleberry, who seems to picture God as a cosmic bellhop, but the logic strikes a responsive cord in us. If God cannot deliver the goods then prayer becomes, at worst, a waste of our time—which may explain why many of us pray so infrequently—or, at best, a polite tip of the hat in God's direction as we go about our business.

But Emmanuel is the Holy One's name, says Matthew, and Emmanuel is not a God of power. Emmanuel, however, is a God who can weep as well as laugh; in him the vagaries of life are no longer outside the divine experience. Emmanuel is a God who is with us, present and attentive.

Is that of significance? I cannot answer for you. But I know there are times in my life when what matters most is having someone to listen, someone who cares what I am going through. I need someone—not to bail me out—but to be attentive; someone who *knows* what it is like and can really be there for me.

Flying back from Tampa recently, I paged through the airline's flight magazine. I found, to my interest, an article having to do with executive marriages and why they break up. It was the contention of the author that executives are accustomed to manipulating and controlling the business affairs of their companies. They tend to be men and women who feel comfortable holding power, making decisions, and issuing orders. But the author suggested that the reason their marriages break up with such frequency is because they have lost the skill of listening. They find it difficult to allow others to have feelings, much less express them, because emotions fall outside their ken or control. The article argued that the most helpful prescription for the survival of executive marriages is the ability to communicate, which includes the ability to listen and hear what another is feeling as well as saying.

The willingness to listen sensitively, however, is important not only for marriages; it is important for the many arenas in which human relationships occur. Recently, I was in a seminary library looking up a reference for this manuscript. My time was short. I was in a hurry. I did not want to be interrupted. You can imagine my frustration when I saw one of the seminarians, a former student of mine, coming over to me. We had not seen each other for several years. I could feel a flush of impatience wash over me as he sat down. He obviously wanted to talk. It was nice to see him again but I had no time for idle chatter. I did not welcome his interruption and was not really interested in what he had to say, but I settled back ready to do my civil duty. He wanted to tell me that he had just learned he was dying of cancer.

The world is filled with people like me who are looking for successful, efficient, robust, no-nonsense messiahs who have no time for weakness or interruptions from folks with problems. But (thank God!) the one who showed up was Emmanuel—one who had the time and the empathy to listen to people pour out their heartaches. Had my friend been able to read my mind, he would never have said what he did. He would not have wasted my time. I am grateful that he could not read in my facial expression all that was going on in my head. But even if he had been able to read the telltale signs in those first moments of our meeting, he could still have said, "Nobody knows the trouble I've seen, nobody knows but Jesus." And the good news is that Jesus does know because his name is Emmanuel. He has been to the front and seen combat. Emmanuel is a God who knows what it means to be vulnerable, weak, defenseless. Emmanuel is a God who has taken off the clerical collar and joined the troops as a foot soldier slugging it out in the trenches. He was born in a barn as a helpless babe with the hint of scandal about him.

Emmanuel reminds us that we are doing business with a God who can listen and hear us. Therefore, not only does praying make sense, but so also the living of our flawed lives. We can receive them as a divine gift without apology or pretense.

All of this is simply to say that when Christmas rolls around again, we dare not approach it as though it is old hat. We cannot assume that we understand the familiar scene, or that the simple story, told so many times that we can recite it from memory, holds no mystery or problem for us. When we come to Bethlehem's barn and look into the manger, if we are going to look at all, we must do so on biblical terms. We come, like Matthew's wise men or Luke's shepherds, humbly and with amazement, laying aside our fond preconceptions, and gaze with wonder at this child. For his name shall be called Emmanuel, that is, God with us.

3

Co-Creators with God

The problem, of course, with believing in God's omnipotence is that, pushed to its theoretical limits, the Almighty becomes an arbitrary, if not cruel, tyrant who allows evil to exist in the world. The divine mandate could prevent evil but does not. The difficulty in such a doctrine becomes manifest when we read the newspaper. The reality of tragedy, wars, and famine press the question, "If God is almighty, then why does the Holy One permit evil in the world?" The sheer magnitude of the Holocaust has raised grave questions about the adequacy of orthodoxy's characterization of God as omnipotent. Satan, in Archibald MacLeish's play, "J.B.," taunts,

> If God is God He is not good,
> If God is good He is not God;
> Take the even, take the odd,
> I would not sleep here if I could.[3]

The devilish dilemma has it: If God is good, then God cannot be in complete control; otherwise there would be no evil in the world. But if God is in charge, then the Almighty must bear full responsibility for human suffering. The divine buck stops with the Commander-in-Chief. The press releases about divine goodness must, therefore, be read with skepticism. Evil is clearly in evidence on this planet. It would appear that, at best, God is an absentee landlord.

But before we conclude that God is either demonic or dead, as Richard Rubenstein has done, let us, for the duration of this chapter, examine another possibility—a possibility that is seen by looking again at the conversation between Gabriel and Mary.

In the sixth month the angel Gabriel was sent from God to a city of Galilee named Nazareth, to a virgin betrothed to a man whose name was Joseph, of the house of David; and the virgin's name was Mary. And he came to her and said, "Hail, O favored one, the Lord is with you!" But she was greatly troubled at the saying, and considered in her mind what sort of greeting this might be. And the angel said to her, "Do not be afraid, Mary, for you have found favor with God. And behold, you will conceive in your womb and bear a son, and you shall call his name Jesus. He will be great, and will be called the Son of the Most High; and the Lord God will give to him the throne of his father David, and he will reign over the house of Jacob forever; and of his kingdom there will be no end" (Luke 1:26-35).

The first thing that stands out in the conversation is the picture of *possibilities* that Gabriel paints. God's envoy comes to Mary with an offer that staggers the human imagination. God promises a king who will inherit the throne of the beloved David and who will establish a kingdom that will stand long after the mountains have crumbled into the sea. Sorrow and sighing, weeping and dying will be no more, and no good thing will be withheld in the realm later envisioned by New Testament writers (cf. Revelation 21). So magnificent will this king be, Gabriel exclaims, that he will be called "Holy," "Son of the Most High."

The offer itself tells us something about the Most High. It portrays a divine generosity of unimaginable proportions. It tells us in graphic language that God is good. The Most High wants the very best for us. With God you go first class all the way! No effort will be spared on our behalf. Every avenue to God's bounty will be opened. Even the desert will become a highway for God's goodness. Every valley shall be lifted up, and every mountain and hill made low. The uneven ground shall become level, and the rough places a plain. The glory of the Lord is to be revealed, and all flesh shall see it together. God is Good; with a capital "G."

Jesus is the assurance of this. If it is not immediately apparent at his birth, it is in his death. When the apostle Paul looks at the cross, he reasons: If God did not spare his own Son, will he not give us everything else necessary for our well-being? (cf. Romans 8:32) His argument is convincing.

Even when we encounter the "No" of God, it is only that we may grow into a more mature relationship with our Patron. Job's experience with the Most High comes to mind. Job approaches the throne of Grace with a preconceived idea of the way life is, or at least, ought to be. He assumes this to be a moral universe in which morality is defined by good guys winning and bad guys losing. Because he is good, he ought not suffer. So he lays his complaint before God, who, he imagines, wears a white hat and demands justice. But God responds in silence! Chapter after chapter, God turns away in silence because the Holy One is not interested in Job's preconception of the way things *ought* to be. No reasons are offered Job for his suffering because God wants to bring him into a new reality. The real world is not ordered by Job's preconception of the way things *ought* to be. The new reality is that life contains mystery and absurdity. Job discovers that life is not reducible to his understanding or comprehension. Indeed, God comes to him as the Enemy, destroying his adolescent idol of justice in order that Job can come to know the Most High as the God of Grace.

By the end of the story, Job understands who his enemy is: God. But he also sees that it is God who gives him his life without reasons for doing so, who gives him the miraculous opportunity of living without justifying that opportunity to him or without his having earned it. Job is lifted to a totally new level of awareness. He is amazed at the miracle of life given him, with all the joys and sorrows that come with it, yet without any more of an explanation of the one than of the other. Job, therefore, no longer regards his existence, his possessions, or his lot in life, as being the result of his deserving—good or bad. He sees his life, rather, as a gift of grace, offered with no explanation attached, a gift that is as much of a mystery as is his suffering. He understands neither why he should suffer nor why he should have been called to live at all. Both are mysteries. In the end, he lives not by answers but by amazement.

Throughout the Bible, God is portrayed as wanting only one thing: a chance to dance with us. Scripture speaks of it as God's righteousness. It is, in fact, God's goodness, and planet Earth is sprinkled with its tokens. Our lives are crowned with its glory.

33

So what else is new? This all sounds very traditional. Orthodox theology has taught it for centuries. Why repeat it? Because it bears repeating! The goodness of God is part of the church's witness. It is written across some page of every believer's experience and if, indeed, it is part of your story and mine, we cannot ignore what we know to be true. The taunting rhyme goes: "If God is good, he is not God. . . . " But one thing we know: God is good! Speaking out of his own experience, Paul declares, "We *know* that in everything God works for good . . . " (Romans 8:28). The response of the community of faith over the years is to say, "Right on!" When we speak out of our experience of God's goodness, we have to add our "Amen!"

The question, then, becomes: If God is good, does it mean that the Most High is not all powerful? Could it be that omnipotence is not an essential attribute of God?

At least in the stories that Luke and Matthew give us, the authors do not appear to think so. They portray the goodness of God, but say little about omnipotence.

Let Luke continue his story:

> And Mary said to the angel, "How shall this be, since I have no husband?" And the angel said to her, "The Holy Spirit will come upon you, and the power of the Most High will overshadow you; therefore, the child to be born will be called holy, the Son of God." . . . And Mary said, "Behold, I am the handmaid of the Lord; let it be to me according to your word" (Luke 1:34-35,38).

Luke focuses our attention on Mary and her cooperation. Matthew, as we have seen, focuses on the helpless infant, whom he claims should be seen as God with us and called, "Emmanuel." Both accounts should give us pause and cause us to reflect. God has no intention of overpowering us; the Holy One comes on stage as one needing to be nurtured and nursed. Had it not been for the loving care of his mother Mary, and the tender devotion of his father Joseph, the baby would not have survived and the Incarnation would have been thwarted. The story is told to impress on us the fact that there was nothing certain about the Incarnation. Whatever else we may say about it, God was clearly risking the enterprise on the cooperation of Mary and the devotion of Joseph. Without these, Jesus would have remained only a longing in God's heart. Without these, God's hopes would have been frustrated. Without the willingness of Mary and Joseph to share in God's dream, there would be no need to remember, much less celebrate Christmas.

All this suggests that there is a vulnerable side to God. The Holy One comes among us with a certain fragility. Love has a soft underbelly, even God's love. To love is always to risk being rejected. There are no guarantees; there are only possibilities.

This vulnerable side of God is also noticed by Old Testament writers. Look again at how they tell the story of the Exodus and the events leading up to it (Exodus 3 and 4). Incredibly, Israel's faith was built on a story that featured God *negotiating* the terms of Moses' job description.

Yahweh's compassion for the enslaved Hebrews is the central theme of the story. Yet God's desire to free them had to wait until a person could be found *willing* to stand up to Pharaoh. God had this vision of a special people—chosen, not for privilege but for responsibility—and, in a conversation similar to the one between Gabriel and Mary, the divine intent is laid before Moses. We can forgive Moses his lack of enthusiasm for God's proposition as he makes first one excuse and then another, for the plan puts him at great risk with the powers that be. Moses does not seem to be afflicted with a martyr complex. Therefore, God has to bargain with Moses, certainly not a requirement for an omnipotent Sovereign, who could dictate terms and demand unconditional surrender.

To say that God limits the divine power is to beg the question and miss the point: God chooses to come among us as One *not* characterized by omnipotence. We are left to wonder what would have been the outcome if Moses had decided *against* being a servant of the Lord.

Note too, how the storytellers follow Israel's national ambition through the Old Testament. Israel wanted to be somebody, taking her place among the great and powerful nations of the Mediterranean basin. Under the leadership of her kings, she sought to gather wealth, exercise influence, and be the envy of the world. But one after another, the prophets of the Lord, reporting for duty before the divine summons, had to stand up to her ambitious dreams, first to woo her, then to cajole her, and finally to threaten her. Being an all-powerful nation was not part of God's plan. The relationship was characterized by a constant contest of wills, a struggle between God's intention and the willingness of these people to bear the divine image.

So it is that when the New Testament stories are told, we are not surprised to find God with yet another great idea. This one involves Jesus, and the plan unfortunately requires Jesus to sacrifice his life for the sake of others. Working out the details of the proposal inconveniently interrupts a promising career for Jesus as a healer, teacher, or magician. We must wonder what would have happened had he decided on a vocation as a doctor or a professor—possibilities which, in hindsight, must have looked very appealing in the Garden of Gethsemane where, it is clear, the thought of sacrifice had lost its appeal. Jesus did not want to die.

And the whole operation began with that conversation recorded by Luke for us between the angel of the Lord and Mary, the young maiden. With a little inspired imagination, we can read between the lines. Gabriel speaks:

> Mary, God's been at it again. This time he has really outdone himself. The Most High wants to visit his people and assure them once and for all that his goodness can be trusted. He cares about all of you, but feels so removed. The Holy One would like to come live with you awhile and offer his love and concern. But, Mary, even heaven has its limitations! God has no way of being with you in person unless he comes as a human being, which means he has to be born into your world as a baby. Those are the rules. And there's no way even God can get around them. He's stuck unless some woman will allow him to be born through her. That's where you come in Mary! What do you say?

Gabriel, of course, may have had a southern accent or spoken with a slight lisp—I do not know—and Luke never heard of the debate about sexist language. What this Gospel story offers for our consideration is the picture of a dynamic relationship between God and us—between divine invention, on the one hand, and human intention, on the other.

It does not portray the relationship as that of a marionette whose strings are pulled by a puppeteer in order to make it dance,

36

offering only the appearance of free choice. Rather, it suggests that life is an experience somewhat similar to that of playing chess with a Grand Master. The Master opens. We make our move. Again it is the Grand Master's turn. After some thought he makes his move—but only after we have made ours. Indeed, the game plan of the Grand Master is dependent upon our moves and can only be determined in response to them.

There is, of course, no way we can defeat a Grand Master of chess. He is far too experienced for us. But how he wins cannot be known in advance because his moves cannot be predetermined. That is what keeps the game interesting—both for us and for the Grand Master.

What this means, therefore, is that we can work against God. Or, like Mary, we can open ourselves to the possibilities of being called as co-creators with God in providing a home for the Most High. Luke's story suggests that God is not the only one responsible in the creative enterprise. The story leads us to believe that we too have a part to play in building the kingdom of God.

By revealing the conversation between Mary and Gabriel, Luke makes it clear that we have been called into partnership with God. We cannot, therefore, sit back and pray, ''God's will be done,'' as if we had no responsibility for bringing it about. The nativity stories of both Luke and Matthew call us to pay attention to the seemingly insignificant hunches and almost overlooked ideas that the Holy One throws our way like seed cast broadside in the wind—seed seeking root on the earth, strewn by an unseen Hand. Wherever love and justice are conceptualized in our world by the Spirit, it is for us to nurture and nurse them. These stories remind us of our responsibility for divine incarnations and our parental accountability before God.

The possibilities of the divine vision become evident in the miracles of Jesus, as do the opportunities for human cooperation in sharing that vision—for example, the feeding of the five thousand (Matthew 14:13-21). There is the crowd, hungry and tired at the end of a long day. God's compassion stands in the wings ready and willing to fill their stomachs, but not even God can feed five thousand mouths without someone's hands to do it.

Furthermore, someone has to shop for groceries and set the table for dinner. That is, someone has to have the bright idea of having a picnic on the lawn and then offering his or her services.

God's compassion for the crowd will be frustrated unless, and until, someone conceives the idea of feeding so many people.

For most of us, such an idea would be inconceivable. "We don't have enough food," we might say. "All we can round up are five loaves and two fish. The stores are closed and everyone is tired. Send them home." Along with the disciples, we would suffer from a massive lack of imagination and see only the obvious problems. By focusing our attention on them, we would fail to see the possibilities.

The miracle story seems to assume that, although God may have been ready to serve a seven-course meal, it could not take place until the light went on in Jesus' imagination. Jesus saw himself as a channel for God's abundance. "Together," he reasoned, "we can feed these people." Not until then could God minister to their needs. With Jesus as co-creator, the crowd was fed, with enough doggie bags left over to fill twelve baskets!

It is generally assumed that miracles are the business of an omnipotent God. It goes with the job description. A miracle is something that God alone does, a mighty act that only the Almighty can accomplish. Something amazing happens, and it is attributed to God's intervention. Dead people are brought back to life. The deaf are made to hear. People who are lame suddenly begin to walk and dance. The sea is calmed and water becomes a surface upon which Jesus and Peter can walk. Food is multiplied to feed the waiting crowd, and water is turned into wine.

But why is it, then, that in all of these Bible stories *Jesus*, not God, is the one credited with the miracle? Turning water into wine, for example (John 2:1-10). That the water became wine— that the molecules were altered in such a way as to transform water chemically into wine—is obviously the Creator's doing, not Jesus'. Why then, is Jesus credited with the miracle?

I submit it is because he dared to act on the basis of a remarkably creative assumption. He risked serving water to the steward of the feast *believing that it could become wine*. He lived "as though. . . ." Water into wine? Ridiculous, we would say. But that is the miracle: *Jesus did not think it was ridiculous*. Nor impossible! He dared it. If God had failed to turn the molecules of water into wine, that would not have diminished Jesus' miracle one iota. For Jesus, the miracle was daring to believe all things are possible with God and living as though . . . it were true.

If we have faith as a mustard seed, he promised, nothing will be impossible to us. He was saying that if we dare to dream and risk a miracle, no one can own us, nothing can restrict us. Impossibilities cannot define us. The point of daring to live as though . . . is that we are not confined to the limitations of what is. If God does not see the exciting possibilities, that is God's problem, not ours. Our miracle is daring to risk being outrageously creative with our lives.

"I'm not concerned with ideas which are merely true," Alfred North Whitehead once told his students. "Come to me with ideas that are interesting." Christ might well say something similar to us. We can sense the frustration in Jesus when he looked out over the crowd and exclaimed, "O faithless and perverse generation, how long am I to be with you? How long am I to bear with you?" (Matthew 17:17). Living with dull, unimaginative, shortsighted, safe people must have been a drag for such an impossibly creative person—someone so in touch with God's dreams.

I happen to believe there is still a market for dreams and that our lives are energized by them. Some years ago, I asked a group of senior high young people to express poetically their understanding of life. One of the group contributed these words:

Why do you sit there silent?
For sanity's sake, can't you say anything?
Something real,
Anything before I drown in a sea of nursery rhymes.
Not a tin hallelujah that will rust and sink—
Something that will live.
Something like a dream.

Someone may taunt, "You'll need more than dreams to live on!" Aye! But if they be *God's* dreams, and if we dare to dream them, miracles can happen. To be a co-creator with God is to be a believer in dreams—God's dreams.

I think of a young sex offender who had no hope of being paroled from prison because a parole required that he have a job waiting for him and an employer who would vouch for his rehabilitation. But there was no way of finding either. He had no friends on the outside to secure that job or talk to prospective employers. It was a classic "catch 22."

Then a young woman, a dreamer who did not know the meaning of the word *impossible*, heard about him. She assumed water could be turned to wine and lived as though it were true. She spent six months running down job offers until she found an employer who was willing to take a chance on him. Single-handedly, she obtained his parole because she dared to dream. The light went on in her imagination. It gave God a chance to act and a new beginning was conceived. A new life was given birth. As with Mary, there was no way on Earth for God to create that new life until someone was willing to let the idea become flesh and blood in their thinking.

Luke's nativity narrative is not just a once-upon-a-time child's story to be read at Christmas. It is, rather, a biblical commentary on life and the nature of the world in which we live. In a hundred different ways the word of the Lord comes to us and says: The Most High has a great idea. God's love for the world wants to become flesh in you. The divine dream desires to incarnate itself through you. Sometimes we find that word embarrassing, as did Mary. Sometimes we find the "great idea" inconvenient, as did Mary. But always our consent is requested, as was Mary's.

The French philosopher Jean-Paul Sartre once observed that we are condemned to freedom. But so also is God condemned to our freedom. God is dependent on our decision and our actions. The Most High not only takes our choices into account as a Grand Master does when he plans his next move; but, indeed, our choices define the reality out of which his next move is created. God's will unfolds in response to the possibilities that we provide. Without them, God cannot move. By conceiving of God as almighty, we may be guilty of taking advantage of a colossal cop-out and shirking our human responsibility. Fortunately, Jesus simplifies our ethical responsibility before God by instructing us to love our neighbor. When we love someone or act out of concern for their well-being, we provide God with the stuff of which the kingdom of God is made. Without such building material, God's hands are tied.

To believe in Christmas, to celebrate Mary's pregnancy and the birth of Jesus every year, is to demonstrate our conviction that we have value as God's co-creators. We are necessary partners in the enterprise of establishing the kingdom of God in this world. Angel voices serenaded the shepherds with, "On earth peace, good will toward men,"(Luke 2:14, KJV) because Mary had said, "Yes." But without her affirmative response, there would have been no singing at all. And, we might add, the shepherds would not have become celebrities. Gospel writers would never have told their tales, and we would be left to shovel manure in our dark, dreary barns.

That message of peace, love, and justice among the people of the Earth could be sung in our world all year long if we, like Mary, were willing to risk opening ourselves to the generative power of God's dreams. Whatever else Luke's account may tell us, it reminds us that God has a lot of great ideas and wants to give them birth through us.

4

The Holy One of Israel

In the last two chapters we have seen how the traditional understanding of God's omnipotence changes when it is illumined by starlight. Now, let us watch in wonder as another of those traditional categories is metamorphosed by the star-struck scene of Emmanuel's birth: God's *holiness.*

Most of us equate holiness with aloofness. Understandably so. The Old Testament stories speak of God as holy and give the concept substance by emphasizing spacial distance. For example, the Ark of the Covenant, which symbolized the Divine presence, was housed in the temple Holy of Holies, segregated from worshipers. It was not to be touched by mere mortals, lest they die. The Ark itself was holy and, therefore, protected by a taboo that prevented people from getting too close and becoming familiar with the sacred artifact. A priesthood was necessary to stand between the proletariat and God, serving to prevent both injury to the people and affront to Yahweh. Even the name of God was sacrosanct. Accidental pronunciation of it by profane lips was prevented by substituting other vowel sounds for the ones originally intoned. Instead of "Yahweh," the sacred name became "Adonai," or "The Lord," and later "Jehovah."

No wonder that when the prophet Isaiah recounted his vision of God, he did so in terms that can only be interpreted as transcendent. He spoke of the Lord as sitting upon a throne,

> Above him stood the seraphim; each had six wings: with two he covered his face, and with two he covered his feet, and with two he flew. And one called to another and said: "Holy, holy, holy is the LORD of hosts; the whole earth is full of his glory." And the foundations of the thresholds

shook at the voice of him who called, and the house was filled with smoke (Isaiah 6:2-4).

So graphic was Isaiah's description of his vision that it has continued to shape the church's understanding and representation of God's holiness to the present. Consequently, God's holiness denotes divine purity, which means separation from the profane muck and grime of the world.

Once, when flying down to see Grandma, my little daughter Susan asked, as the plane climbed above the cloud castles and broke into radiant sunlight, "Is God up here?" It is a child's question born of a child's understanding of God. Yet many adults never outgrow the conception of God as the Old Man in the sky. When the first Russian cosmonaut returned from his flight into space, he tauntingly boasted that he found no trace of God up there.

While it is true most thinking Christians would not expect to look for God up—or even out—there, the fact remains that our concept of holiness presupposes God is, in one way or another, removed from us and the scenes of our scandalous endeavors. Certainly, Susan would not have thought to look for God in a manure-ridden barn. Holiness and purity go together. And purity requires separation from worldly taint—not only in the mind of a child but for most of us. We think so little of our world and ourselves that any thought of God must be in terms totally apart from anything worldly. If we think of God at all, the Holy One is thought of in terms of unapproachable majesty.

That is, until Luke picks up pen and puts it to paper:

> In those days a decree went out from Caesar Augustus that all the world should be enrolled. This was the first enrollment, when Quirinius was governor of Syria. And all went to be enrolled, each to his own city. And Joseph also went up from Galilee, from the city of Nazareth, to Judea, to the city of David, which is called Bethlehem, because he was of the house and lineage of David, to be enrolled with Mary, his betrothed, who was with child. And while they were there, the time came for her to be delivered. And she have birth to her first-born son and wrapped him in swaddling cloths, and laid him in a man-

ger, because there was no place for them in the inn (Luke 2:1-7).

Born in a barn! Of questionable parentage! Held and adored by dirty shepherds with dung under their fingernails! With sledgehammer blows, all of the traditional taboos are broken. Our understanding of holiness is forever altered. Any idea of aloofness has to go. We are left with an understanding of holiness that embodies, not spatial distance, but the *otherness* of God—other than anything we could have imagined, other than anything we would have expected, perhaps even other than anything we want.

Dietrich Bonhoeffer speaks of this babe born in a stable as God's birthday wish come true. The Holy One's most burning desire was not to remain with the adoring angels, where the latest press clippings and heavenly polls all confirmed the Sovereign's popularity. No, God's birthday wish was to be in and with the world. And, it must be noted, not a world that had been sanitized for the divine visitation. There were no secret service agents to check it out and make the visit safe. And, clearly, there was no bullet-proof limousine to take the expectant couple to the barn. Not a world of antiseptic splendor offering a "red carpet" welcome for a prestigious potentate. It was the world you and I see every evening on the nightly news—a world of scandal and dirt, common laborers and corrupt government officials.

Yet that is the world God wanted to be with because it beat staying in heaven with all those angels. " . . . And his name will be called 'Emmanuel,' " Matthew insists—that is, God with us.

Now this presents us with something of a dilemma, and we again find ourselves faced with another crisis of faith. Either we must conclude that God has no class—as though we were authorities on divine style, qualified to judge what really is appropriate for a divine disclosure—or we have to accept Emmanuel as *God's* normative definition of holy. That which is holy, by divine design, is not spiritual but, *radically* worldly and totally human!

At issue is our own relationship to things worldly. What we assume about God predisposes us to relate to ourselves and our world in one way or another. If God is high and lifted up, the tendency is to spiritualize religion and separate ourselves from secular concerns. A piety that seeks purity is an attempt to remain free of worldly taint.

But with the birth of Jesus a religion of remarkable worldliness was born. Not only do we have need of God, but God has just as much need of us. In Jesus we see the bonding of the divine and the human, the sacred and the secular. The distinction between them has been erased because in Jesus the one can no longer be known apart from the other. In that baby born in a barn and lighted by a star, two worlds have been fused. The alloy is called the kingdom of God.

So as long as God is understood as "high and lifted up," go-betweens will be necessary to represent the divine interests and human concerns. Preachers and prophets will always find employment. Unfortunately, in the American religious tradition, conceived as it was in the frontier spirit and nurtured by a healthy dose of rugged individualism, we find it very easy to disregard God's spokespersons. With no fear of lightning striking, we say to prophets and preachers alike, "I don't agree with you. That's your opinion, but I see things differently. I can't agree with you, and I'm certainly not going to let someone tell me what to do!" We thereby dismiss the go-betweens with a fair amount of ease.

But what do we say to Emmanuel? God with us . . . in a barn? For example, how do we say that concern for the poverty-plagued shepherds is a matter of opinion? How can I say to Emmanuel that my child's education is more important than that of the kid in the ghetto?

Or, how do you say to Emmanuel that it is more important for you to live in a $100,000 house than it is to provide for public housing, and therefore you will vote against a tax increase because its passage would mean cutting back of your vacation this year? In a world where we, who are 6 percent of the world's population, consume 40 percent of the world's goods while three quarters of its population goes to bed hungry at night, how do we say to Emmanuel, "I can't afford to tithe?"

Later, as an adult, Jesus would himself delineate the ethic that is connected to this radical redefinition of holiness. To love God, says Jesus, is to love the least of these poor souls who are hungry, homeless, imprisoned, or naked (cf. Matthew 25:31-46). That covers a lot of uncomfortable ground! But the New Testament writers are adamant. If we cannot love our needy neighbor, whom we have seen, we cannot love God, whom we have not seen. The logic is devastating. John pulls no punches when he says that anyone who claims to love God while hating his brother is a liar (1 John 4:20). Not uninformed, not short-sighted, not ignorant. A barefaced *liar!* In most circles, "them's fightin' words." The category of divine holiness, like that of omnipotence, is turned on its ear—our ear.

To take on the name of Christ as a "Christian" is to be radically bonded to those who have been overlooked by the distributors of this world's goodies, those who have been born and must live in the "barns" of this world. For us who assume that Jesus is the Christ, reaching out to those less fortunate is the ethical imperative. This means doing what Jesus did by becoming involved in the lives of those who are regarded as less than beautiful by the usual standards of society—economic, social, and moral.

That point seems dangerously close to being missed by many of us as Christians in this country. Today, multitudes of our people look upon their spiritual journeys as a religious quest in search of personal fulfillment. The huge array of nondenominational parachurch organizations and Bible study movements that have captured the allegiance of millions offer a personalized perspective of the gospel story that panders to this market. The emergence in the late 1960s of the Charismatic Renewal Movement has further individualized the Christian faith.

In the 1980s the religious landscape has been enlarged to include a rapidly growing number of churches that do not identify themselves with any of the historic denominations. All are aggressively seeking converts. Even in mainline churches the emphasis today is on "evangelism," which functionally means a head-to-head competition for winning the allegiance of those who may already be interested in the more traditional institutionalized forms of religion. In short, it becomes a game of musical chairs— or pews, with happy hymn singers merely moving from church to church and not from the streets into the sanctuary. The drive toward self-preservation is, in the end, stronger than the desire for social change.

Whether because of fear or tiredness or boredom or change in the national temperament, the causes of the sixties have given way to different priorities. Virtually every public opinion poll

46

comes up with essentially the same results: The concern for social justice and human rights is losing ground in the search for an individualized spirituality and numerical growth.

A majority of Presbyterians, for example, have traditionally believed that it is important to place "equal emphasis on winning people to Christ and changing society in his name."[4] But that majority is significantly smaller today than it was fifteen years ago. In a decade-and-a-half those members who believed that changing society in Christ's name was important slipped from 79 percent to less than 55 percent. Among its ministers the slippage was from 90 percent to less than 75 percent. Translating the statistics into a theological observation: It seems to suggest that those of us who are Presbyterians increasingly do not believe that the Messiah was really born in a barn, nor that as his followers we are called to take seriously this world as the arena for displaying the concerns of the Most High God for equality and justice. It even suggests, dare I say, that we are waiting for a Messiah who offers us a better deal!

The world is full of Christians who are hoping for a better deal from God. We sometimes assume God to be a heavenly genie who is there to grant our every wish or a divine rabbit's foot to be hung around our necks in times of impending danger. More to the point, we are offended by a God who has no class. We are embarrassed by weakness and offended by suffering when they become characteristics of the divine holiness. We want a god who is at least exalted, if not almighty—someone to whom we can look up.

Historically, this desire among Christians has been labeled the "docetic heresy." Docetism comes from the Greek word, *dokeo*, which means, "it seems." The heresy taught that Jesus only *seemed* to be human. In reality, he was eternally divine and had only temporarily assumed a human disguise in order to masquerade among us.

So prevalent was the docetic heresy in the early church that one of the reasons for the formulation of the Apostles' Creed was to combat its influence. When the Creed affirms that Jesus was, "born of a virgin, suffered under Pontius Pilate, was crucified, dead, and buried. He descended into hell . . . ," it is attempting to underline his true humanity: He was born, he hurt, he died, he really was one of us. No masquerade. No pretense. No ifs, ands, or buts about it!

It is this heresy, so persistent in the life of the church, which has surfaced again in our time. Believers usually have no trouble with the divinity of Jesus. Almost compulsively, we have sought to put him on a pedestal and worship him. Never mind that he never set himself up as the focus for our adulation but always pointed beyond himself to God. "Why do you call me good?," he once said to a would-be admirer. "No one is good but God alone" (Mark 10:18). But we have great difficulty letting Jesus come down from his pedestal and walk among us as an honest-to-God human being.

So we cut our Messiah from the same piece of cloth as John Wayne. Better yet, Superman—a hero in the cause of justice. A clever fellow, resourceful, and witty. Appropriately shy and modest yet able to leap tall buildings in a single bound, faster than a speeding bullet. And, of course, more powerful than a locomotive—or the powers of death. God-like? Yes! No problem. But not just your garden variety, ordinary type human being with the disgusting scent of scandal about him!

So the pernicious docetic heresy is alive and well today among religious folks. Theologians now call it "Messianic Triumphalism." But whatever it is called, it spawns a variety of telltale slogans imprinted on bumper stickers that cause, no doubt, many an innocent motorist to drive to his or her death trying to read the blasted things: "Church-going families are happier families!," "It pays to tithe!," "Prayer works!," "Jesus is the answer!" We want a Savior who has answers and can solve all problems if only we will "take it to the Lord in prayer"—a Savior who can deliver us from our distress and overcome our difficulties, One who rides to the rescue with the cavalry or at least knows a shortcut around Calvary.

But it is precisely our would-be Rescuer, the Hero of whom we are so proud, that scandalizes us by flaunting his vulnerability before us. We yearn for a Gospel story that accentuates the positive and eliminates the negative, responding to the deep desire within us to escape the embarrassment of our own humanity.

"So, what is the point," you ask, "in emphasizing Christ's scandalous humanity?"

The answer is disarmingly simple. The world is full of triumphant messiahs. They are a dime a dozen. From religious leaders who point their accusing fingers at us from the lofty heights of purity or slam their pulpits in dogmatic certainty, to a national administration that espouses a policy of God, guns, and guts—they are all around us, attracting a crowd of convinced and committed disciples. A Jim Jones who gathers a People's Temple or an Ayatollah Khomeini bent on establishing an Islamic empire are simply the more obvious examples. All have one thing in common: They have the Key. They have the Answers. They know how to solve the problem. It is that subtle—and sometimes not so subtle—arrogance that draws lines around those who have the answer and those who do not, those who have seen the light and those still in darkness, those who stand on the inside of the circle and those who belong on the outside. Protestants are sure Catholics are idolaters in their veneration of Mary. Christians are sure that a Hindu understanding of God is pagan. Democrats are convinced the country will fail under Republican leadership. And you cannot play ball with the St. Louis Cardinals if you wear a New York Mets uniform.

Football is the great American spectator sport, I believe, because it best calls up our neurotic need to identify with power and grind those who differ with us into the ground. Vince Lombardi, coach of the Green Bay Packers, articulated those desires when he declared, "Winning isn't the main thing. It's the *only* thing." For us, the name of the game is winning—gaining and exercising power. It is the means by which we establish our identity as individuals and as a nation.

"I'm a sucker for hero worship," Ronald Reagan once said. Most politicians at least pay lip service to heroic behavior, but Reagan sounded the theme perhaps more insistently than any other president. One of the top priorities of his administration was to increase our military budget—the largest in peacetime history, it must be noted, and at the expense of domestic programs to aid the homeless, the hungry, and the poor. The aim was clearly to build our military might until we were unquestionably the toughest kid on the street. We invaded the tiny island of Grenada like an adolescent flexing his muscles before the bathroom mirror. We tried to bully the sovereign nation of Nicaragua, demanding that it bow before our will and say "Uncle!" In our view of things, power is measured by beating the other person, team, or nation.

49

Our identity is secured by being stronger and more successful than the competition.

We live in a world of walls. We have built fences behind which we live. You are either on my side of the fence or you are not one of us. It is a world of "us" and "them." And if you are not one of us, then I am suspicious of you and view you, at best, as an outsider; and, at worst, as an enemy.

Jesus was born and lived in exactly that kind of a fractured world. Jews and Samaritans, Pharisees and sinners, the Chosen and the Gentiles. But Jesus destroyed the walls by refusing to honor the distinctions. In his birth, his lifestyle, and his death, he exhibited a divine determination to share a common and quite mundane humanity with us. He needed a mother's milk and a father's example. He desired a drink of water from an outcast Samaritan woman and the companionship of a score of disciples. In the Gospel stories, Jesus displays an incredibly different kind of power. Rather than trying to secure himself against the other person, Jesus opens himself to them. He does not compete with them nor try to argue them down. He makes himself vulnerable to them by admitting that he is not self-sufficient. He presents himself as a person who recognizes his own limitations, needs, and dependency upon others. He acknowledges before God and the world that others have gifts that he needs.

Jesus was a person so secure within himself that he did not have to belittle, intimidate, or humiliate the other person. He was a man of great stature, a person of great size. But size, for Jesus, was not measured by controlling another individual's life or turf. Rather, it was understood by him as the ability to open himself to the influence of another person and, thereby, enabling *both* to become bigger, better individuals. The greater the other person was allowed to become, the greater Jesus became.

The Gospel stories seem to suggest that holiness as we have traditionally understood it is not conducive to building community. It does not, indeed cannot, bring us together. Holiness, in any traditional understanding of the term, has to go. It cannot contribute to "peace on earth, good will toward people." To live in splendid isolation, in self-sufficient grandeur, does not break down the barriers that separate us. Holy messiahs may attract crowds, but they do not overcome our alienation. They simply create another competing group and open up yet another rift on our already fractured planet.

Had it not been for Jesus' helplessness as a baby, his neediness as an adult, his vulnerability in death, we and the Most High God would still be on opposite sides of the fence. The statement that "In Christ God was reconciling the world to himself," (2 Corinthians 5:19) has little or nothing to do with the forgiveness of our sins. It has rather to do with the fact that Jesus did not count equality with God a thing to be grasped but truly emptied himself and became one of us (Philippians 2:7). Jesus took off his clerical collar and risked getting decked in the brawl. He risked taking his lumps with the rest of us and, in so identifying with us, tore down the temple curtain that separated the Holy of Holies from the courts of the profane (Mark 15:38). God's holiness destroys the distinctions that separate us from our Creator and each other.

It is when we risk sharing our humanity, with all of its limitations and vulnerability, that community is built. Not through competition and the display of power.

Not too long ago, I attended a sophisticated gathering where food abounded and the drinks flowed freely. The conversation was intellectual, clever, and superficial. Everyone seemed to be having a good time. Across the room was a woman who was obviously the victim of multiple sclerosis. She was having great difficulty keeping the food on her plate, much less getting it to her mouth. And, of course, she was ignored by everyone at the party. It was difficult for her to speak and hard for others to understand her. So she sat there by herself. It brought back uncomfortable memories of those four and a half years when I was without a voice due to spastic dysphonia. I remembered feeling like a ventriloquist's dummy at social gatherings because my wife had to speak for me. I knew the feelings of awkward loneliness, and I could not but think to myself, "God, what courage that woman has!" I wanted to meet her. So I took my plate and joined her in the corner. We sat together and talked—just the two of us. It was a delightful conversation. She was, as I had imagined, a fascinating person—intellectual, clever, and deep. But had it not been for the fact that I, too, had been a cripple, I probably would never have spoken to her and discovered what a delightful human being she is.

When we share our awkwardness, our embarrassments, our

51

fears, our needs, we discover the community of the Kingdom. When Jesus spoke to the outcast Samaritan woman at the well (John 4:5-15), he spoke as a needy Messiah. They talked, just the two of them, about the one thing that really mattered in their lives. Not their accomplishments, not the banal superficialities of the weather, or the ball scores. Jesus was thirsty and he asked her for a drink! They talked about water, living water. They discovered that each had something to give to the other.

If the popularity of religion is on the increase in our society, it may simply be because it is playing upon the docetic desire for a triumphant Messiah, a hero who can offer us a better deal than vulnerability and weakness. We hope for an offer of immunity from prosecution as we face the scandal of our humanity.

I do not mean to depreciate the rise of religious interest in our society. Instinctively, we reach out to something beyond ourselves. Humbled by the awareness of an expanding universe and a life span measured in decades, we sometimes feel overwhelmed by our individual insignificance and seek to align ourselves with some group, cause, or ideology that transcends our own finiteness. It is this universal impulse that lies at the heart of the religious instinct.

But hidden within this natural inclination lies a perverse tendency to enhance our significance at the expense of someone else's. "My dad is better than your dad," we taunted as children. As adults it becomes, "Our free enterprise system is better than their communism," or "We Protestants are more godly than you Catholics." We want to be secure in our significance.

When this inclination toward significance seeks to establish itself by achieving supremacy over others, conflict arises, ranging from family feuds to world wars. And when this attempt is made in the name of God, fanaticism results—holy wars, crusades, purges, inquisitions.

During the early part of this decade, Dean Kelley's book, *Why Conservative Churches Are Growing*,[5] became the manual of arms for mainline church leaders who thought that a bit of zealousness and dogmatic certainty was what was needed to revitalize religion. Numerous renewal programs were launched intended to get back to basics, reclaiming our roots. But as Will Durant once noted, "Certainty is dangerous." In a world where cyanide and megaton might make certainty murderous, Triumphal

Messianism in any form can be dangerous to our health.

For a remedy Jesus, as Messiah, offers us a good dose of human humility. But we are not sure what to do with it—swallow it or gag on it. So we run from it, or deny it by pulling his halo down over our eyes so we will not have to look at it. But the scandal of his humanity rises up every year to haunt us as we celebrate the birth of this baby born in a barn. And therein lies our hope, for the Incarnation will not leave us alone. It not only defines the holiness of God, it defines our humanity as well.

5

The Importance of Being Carnal

In the beginning was the Word, and the Word was with God, and the Word was God. He was in the beginning with God; all things were made through him, and without him was not anything made that was made. In him was life, and the life was the light of men. The light shines in the darkness, and the darkness has not overcome it (John 1:1-5).

The nativity story of John's Gospel is the most philosophical in nature, and its starshine the most cosmic in scope. Yet the overall effect is that the scandal of the Incarnation is all the more stunning. "The Word became flesh and dwelt among us," says John, "full of grace and truth; we have beheld his glory . . ." (John 1:14).

At the root of our word *incarnation* lies the word *carnal*, which the dictionary defines: "In or of the flesh; bodily; material or worldly, not spiritual; having to do with or preoccupied with bodily or sexual pleasures; sensual or sexual." The story of incarnation demands our reflection on the shocking realization that the Most High is preoccupied with bodily, sensual, or sexual pleasures; not spiritual. When God decided to reveal the true nature of divinity, the Holy One did so in a body. God came as a sexual creature. God came *carnally*.

The church has always had trouble accepting that fact. In the early creeds of the church, for example, God was spoken of as having no body, parts, or passions. It was offensive to think of a Supreme Being in those terms. Theologians have been embarrassed by the frank anthropomorphism of the Old Testament, which speaks of God using a body to walk in a garden (Genesis 3:8), smelling incense (Genesis 8:21), and looking at rainbows (Genesis 9:16). Christian art in the Middle Ages pictured Jesus as an effeminate man with a halo adorning his head, all of which obscured the fact that he could command the allegiance of other men, and was physically attractive to women who, the record indicates, flocked around him during his ministry. The church has never had any trouble affirming Jesus as the Son of God with connections in heavenly places, but it has had great difficulty affirming him as a man of the Earth—the Son of Man—a title that completely dropped out of use in the early Christian community. Church officials are usually disturbed if ministerial candidates do not confess Jesus as the Son of God, the second person in the Trinity, but seem to care less about insuring the confession that he is the Son of Man.

If we truly believe that the divine nature was embodied in Jesus, it means taking seriously John's assertion that humanity is, indeed, the essential attribute of the Eternal God. Nor can we afford to forget that when God becomes flesh, it necessarily alters the way we are to understand our carnal nature.

Traditional Christian theology has held that the manner in which the grace of God enters the human experience is through the preaching of God's word and the administration of the church's sacraments. Christian theology has traditionally considered matters of the flesh as less important, and certainly less godly, than things of the mind or spirit. For nineteen hundred years, orthodox thinkers in the Western church have either based their understanding of God on scripture or the tradition of the church. Generally speaking, Protestants have believed that divine truth is revealed in the Bible, a book which has come to be known as the "word of God." Some denominations believe it to be the only infallible rule of "faith and practice," "the unique and authoritative" word of God. What has been true of the Protestant church has also been true in the Roman Catholic tradition. Papal pronouncements, conciliar decisions, and Thomistic thought have become the building blocks for all theological discussion. They are the revealed truth, unique and authoritative for Catholic faith and practice. For mainline western Christians, God's word is a given; either in the church's tradition or in scripture.

It follows, therefore, that Christian truth is not something that believers discover in human, that is carnal, experience, much less within themselves. It is rather something that believers extract from what has already been given to the church.

The procedure for extraction is a rational process whereby ideas are linked together logically, beginning with what is given. The end result is called, a "systematic theology," which proceeds from a basic premise or governing idea, such as the sovereignty of God, salvation by faith, or an ascending reality from natural to spiritual. That this truth can be taught and comprehended by the human mind is a basic assumption underlying the model of Christian ministry that requires an educational standard for its clergy. Truth is thought to be objective. It is "out there." It is external to us. The good reverend is a scholar, a preacher, and a teacher; and he or she has the academic credentials to prove it. Sermons are expositions of scripture, and preaching seeks to instill correct beliefs in the minds of the listeners. The minister knows something by virtue of his or her education that church members do not. The result is unfortunate. Faith formation tends to become a cerebral affair. Intellectual propositions are offered as truth, and accepted by belief.

Historically, religious education in both the Sunday church school and weekday parochial school has been heavy on academic content and short on human experience. It has approached the teaching task as if the faith were a body of facts to be learned, Bible verses to be memorized, theological statements to be understood, names, dates, and events to be grasped. Students were catechized; that is, they were taught correct answers to stipulated questions. A variety of creative means, such as audio-visuals, activities, and colorful pictures are now sometimes employed to carry out this teaching. But no matter how creative the means may be, they are used to teach knowledge *about* the Christian faith. The end result of such education turns out to be learning *about* the Bible, *about* the church, *about* God; but rarely is it a communication of *Christian religious experience*.

Christian educators could well take a page from the teaching manual of the Most High. When it came time for the divine disclosure, another sermon was not offered, nor a new edition of the written Law. No, "the Word became flesh," says John, "and dwelt among us . . . and we have beheld his glory . . . " That is to say, we saw him, we touched him, we experienced him with our senses—this man of grace who was the very Word of God in our midst. We experienced him carnally. The Most High did not offer us more knowledge *about* divine matters. In Jesus we were treated to real, honest-to-God knowledge of the Most High. In him we see the meaning of the words, "created in the image of God," an image which, by divine decree, has been inscribed and fixed within our carnal nature and is, therefore, a part of each one of us.

We can only know God by embracing our own humanity. There is a pervasive inclination among many to deny that flesh enters into the essential definition of human nature, much less that of God. Undoubtedly, the reason we have so much trouble with the humanity of Jesus is because we have such great difficulty with our own. We are embarrassed by it!

Motion picture star Catherine Deneuve was once interviewed after filming a picture in which she had to play some of the scenes nude. Her response is revealing.

> I'm shy, extremely shy. I could never empty my handbag in front of anyone. I find it so excruciating to play nude scenes. For *Belle de Jour*, in the most difficult scenes, to overcome my modesty I had to take a few strong drinks. One must always help oneself to reach where one must go. I got there I hope, but it was hell.
>
> I don't even run around naked in my own house very much. I don't think there are many actresses to whom nude, very explicit physical love scenes come easy. There's a simple reason for female reluctance. Clothes are like a new virginity, but, above all, not that many women are proud of their nude bodies.[6]

True of women! True of men! Not many of us are that proud of our bodies—or our humanity. We are embarrassed by it.

Marilyn Monroe must have had such people in mind when she said, in an interview shortly before her death, "We are all born sexual creatures, thank God, but it's a pity so many people despise and crush this natural gift."[7]

As a result of this embarrassment, the Christian religion has dissected human nature and labeled it "body" and "soul," It has argued that the soul is where the real action is. The soul, we say, is immortal. Long after the body is gone, the soul will live on in eternity. God's only real interest is the soul. The body is a problem, if not *the* problem. Because of this paranoia about the physical, we have spiritualized not only the Holy One but divine grace as well. "Grace" has come to mean God's mercy, which forgives us our sins so that we may enter the kingdom of heaven. Note, too, how frequently we speak of the "kingdom of heaven," rather than the "kingdom of God." In the Old Testament, at least, whenever the reign of God was mentioned, it always referred to a kingdom in this world, not in the sweet by-and-by.

Not only have we split human nature down the middle, we have set it against itself—the body versus the soul. As a result, sex has gotten a bad press from the church for nineteen centuries. Monastic living has become, for some, the religious ideal. If you really want to make it with God, if you really want to be spiritual, you must leave the world, suppress the body, and deny the flesh so that you are free to contemplate the spiritual realities of life.

It is against this kind of spirituality that John's shocking and scandalous assertion is directed. The Word became flesh. Jesus is God *incarnate*, that is to say, Jesus is God in carnal form. God's grace is to be understood *carnally* because that is how it comes to us.

Our own experience verifies John's assertion. Grace—that joyous sense of wholeness and well-being, that sense of belonging, that sense that life is good and everything in it is a gift fresh from the Creator's hand—grace comes to us through the physical senses. It comes to us carnally. We are drawn, for example, to a work of art when our senses commune with it. We respond to its color and form and are uplifted. Spirit speaks to spirit. We hear a theme in a piece of music that touches us deeply. Our being is engaged at its very depths in some unexplainable way. Being touches being. We find joy in holding a piece of pottery in our hands. The form of it feels good and true. Something happens that transcends the rational process. Form communicates to form, sense to sense. The experience of grace can be found in caressing winds on the face, words of friendship, or the touching of flesh by flesh. Ours is a sensuous God. And Jesus is the Son of this God.

The Gospel writer Luke offers us an interesting and revealing story about Jesus, who is a "chip off the Old Block" (Luke 7:36-50). Simon the Pharisee has prepared a banquet for his distinguished guest, Jesus of Nazareth, the holy man of God. The story begins in a thoroughly predictable manner. Simon, a good, upstanding churchman, one of the best educated members of the community and no doubt a civic leader, had invited a distinguished guest to dinner. He probably came home strutting, and announced to his wife, "Guess who's coming to dinner! Jesus, the mighty prophet!"

Probably all of us can reach back into memory and pull out a similar incident when our parents invited the minister to dinner. Mother would bring out the silver service and best table linen. We were instructed to be on our best behavior. The conversation was guarded—nothing too controversial—because, after all, the guest in our home was a spiritual leader. So the dinner that Simon the Pharisee planned was to be in every respect proper. But then there was this disturbance.

> And behold, a woman of the city, who was a sinner, when she learned that (Jesus) was at table in the Pharisee's house, brought an alabaster flask of ointment, and standing behind him at his feet, weeping, she began to wet his feet with her tears, and wiped them with the hair of her head, and kissed his feet, and anointed them with the ointment. Now when the Pharisee who had invited him saw it, he said to himself, "If this man were a prophet, he would have known who and what sort of woman this is who is touching him, for she is a sinner" (Luke 7:37-39).

This, too, could have been predicted. After all, public figures are the targets of demonstrations. But what was unexpected, and indeed most disturbing to Simon, was Jesus' reaction. The spiritual leader did not seem to mind the interruption—nor the attention of the intruder. No doubt Simon wondered who it was who had come to dinner. If a holy man could not recognize a sinner when he saw one, something must be terribly wrong. The woman made a spectacle of herself by falling all over Jesus and kissing his feet. Any of us, in a similar situation, would have been offended by all the touching. Certainly we would have felt awkward at being approached by this gushy, overpainted woman of the street. With studied composure and affected benevolence, we might have responded with a clever putdown, such as, "My dear, go wash *yourself*." We would have expected Jesus to declare her behavior inappropriate, or at least to have disapproved of it by some sort of pained glance at Simon. But he did none of these things. He sat there accepting and—it would seem—enjoying all of her attention.

The record is clear. If Jesus is Emmanuel, that is, God with us, then we must admit ours is a scandalous God who enjoys sensuous experience.

We might, therefore, expect the word of such a God to itself be occasionally erotic as well as sensuous. And, indeed, it is!

> How fair and pleasant you are,
>   O loved one, delectable maiden!
> You are stately as a palm tree,
>   and your breasts are like its clusters.
> I say I will climb the palm tree
>   and lay hold of its branches.
> Oh, may your breasts be like clusters of the vine,
>   and the scent of your breath like apples,
> and your kisses like the best wine
>   that goes down smoothly,
>   gliding over lips and teeth.
> (Song of Solomon 7:6-9)

D.H. Lawrence earned the disapproval of literary critics for writing such as that. "Scandalous!" they said. In his novels he frequently described sensuous encounters between men and women and the experience of grace that can come to us in making love. Lady Chatterly, for example,

> was filled . . . with an unspeakable pleasure, pleasure which has no contact with speech. She felt herself filled with new blood, as if the blood of the man had swept into her veins like a strong, fresh, rousing wind, changing her whole self. All her self felt alive, and in motion, like the woods in spring. She could not but feel that a new breath had swept into her body from the man, and that she was like a forest sloughing with a new, soft wind, sloughing and moving unspoken into bud. All her body felt like the

dark interlacing of the boughs of an oak wood, softly humming in a wind, and humming inaudibly with the myriad . . . unfolding of buds. Meanwhile the birds had their heads laid on their shoulders and slept with delight in the vast interlaced intricacy of the forest of her body.[8]

Beautiful! A description of grace understood carnally. But D.H. Lawrence paid a high price for such writing—for daring to suggest that the body, flesh, sex could reflect anything spiritual or divine. His works were banned in his native England as well as in this country. Yet in the New Testament, this shocking book of tales told in the name of God, we have an uncensored story of another woman who, like Lady Chatterly, received grace from the body of a man—the body of the man, Jesus.

According to Luke (8:42-48), the woman was hemorrhaging. She was healed, not by anything Jesus said to her, but by reaching out and touching him. She touched his body and grace abounded. Grace came to her carnally.

Grace comes to us through our bodies. Remember our experience during the Vietnam war when a certain picture was carried in newspapers and TV news reports all across the country? A North Vietnamese, his hands tied behind him, was standing on a street in Saigon with a South Vietnamese officer holding a gun to his head, just before the trigger was pulled in execution. Television, of course, carried the full horror of it and we saw the victim squeeze his eyes shut just before his head exploded into eternity, saw him collapse like a rag doll onto the pavement, saw his blood draining silently into a pool on the street. Instinctively, our bodies cried out in shock. We gasped and hid our eyes.

Then our minds stepped in and began to fashion a commentary. We rationalized what we had seen. "He was just a North Vietnamese. He was the enemy. He deserved to die because he and his kind were killing our boys. His government endangered our national security."

But our bodies recoiled by instinct. No rationalization could justify what we sensed in the initial shock. In that moment, before the mind stepped in with its commentary, our bodies conveyed to us the word of grace: All human life is sacred. War is blasphemy!

According to Jesus, God makes his sun rise on the good and

on the evil, causes his rain to fall on the just and the unjust (Matthew 5:45). No rationalization there. No differentiation. Our bodies know that truth. Our instinctive body reaction has a reverence for the flesh of all people. Our carnal nature is in tune with God's sense of values even if our minds are not. It is only in the rationalization that the word of grace is lost.

And so the amazing affirmation of the scandal lit by the light of a star is that God trusts the carnal. The Most High trusts the body, trusts the sensual, trusts the sexual. The Holy One has made them a vehicle of divine revelation. Carnality and revelation are not only compatible, says John, they are essential to one another. The Word became flesh—that is, carnal—and dwelt among us, full of grace and truth. God cannot do without the carnal. Nor can we. If the Most High trusts the body, the sensuous, the sexual, the earthy, so can we. We can live joyously in our humanity.

6

The Promise of Life

What does it mean to live in our humanity? Assumptions offered as answers abound. They come from philosophers and poets, motion pictures and Madison Avenue. Everyone, it seems, wants to get into the act. Our image of what being human means is molded for us by the matrix of values, attitudes, and images in which we live. It is shaped by the stories we come to accept as reality.

For example, a television commercial advertises a product which, when added to the wash water, is supposed to make towels and T-shirts soft and fluffy. One of the advantages of using the product, the commercial implies, is that a teenager will run to his mother when he discovers how soft his T-shirts are, give her a hug, and say, "Gee, Mom, I love you." Would that the matter of human relations could be so easily solved! I cannot vouch for the effectiveness of the product in making clothes soft, but I am almost certain that it will have nothing to do with family dynamics. If the reality is anything like our household, the teenager—far from noticing the softness of his clothes—would complain that he had to go to the dryer to get his T-shirts instead of finding them in his dresser drawer.

The commercial illustrates the difference between fact and fancy. What is promised and the fulfillment of the promise are two different things. The Bible, surprisingly, sometimes reflects this same gap between promise and fulfillment. There in its pages is Joshua, standing on the far side of the River Jordan, ready to lead his people into the Promised Land. He psyches them up with a first class pep talk.

"Hereby you shall know that the living God is among

you, and that he will without fail drive out from before you the Canaanites, the Hittites, . . . the Amorites, and the Jebusites" (Joshua 3:10).

That was the fancy. The facts were something different as the records indicate:

> However they did not drive out the Canaanites that dwelt in Gezer: so the Canaanites have dwelt in the midst of Ephraim to this day but have become slaves to do forced labor. . . .
> Manasseh did not drive out the inhabitants of Bethshean and its villages. . . . But the Canaanites persisted in dwelling in that land. When Israel grew strong, they put the Canaanites to forced labor, but did not utterly drive them out.
> And Ephraim did not drive out the Canaanites who dwelt in Gezer; but the Canaanites dwelt in Gezer among them (Joshua 16:10; Judges 1:27-29).

One after another, the lieutenants of Israel tried their hand at driving out the Canaanites: Manasseh, Ephraim, Zebulon, Asher; and all with the same results: "they did not drive them out. . . . "

Several centuries later, when the Old Testament prophet was envisioning the anticipated reign of the Messiah, he told the people that the king would heal the diseases of all the people, restoring sight to the blind, enabling the lame to walk, and unstopping the ears of the deaf (Isaiah 35:5,6). That was the promise and the expectation.

Reality, however, is painted for us by Mark's Gospel:

> They brought to [Jesus] all who were sick or were possessed with demons. And the whole city was gathered together about the door. And he healed many who were sick with various diseases, and cast out many demons. . . . And in the morning, a great while before day, [Jesus] rose and went out to a lonely place, and there he prayed. And Simon and those who were with him pursued him, and they found him and said to him, "Every one is searching for you." [But] he said to them, "Let us go on to the next towns, that I may preach there also; for that is why I came" (Mark 1:32-38).

64

Jesus apparently had no intention of exorcising all of the demons. The kingdom of God described in Isaiah turned out to be, in reality, a land where demons not only dwelt, but where the king had no intention of driving them all out.

These stories of fact and fancy raise the question of God's credibility. What, for example, is the believer in faith-healing to make of the fact that his or her prayers for recovery go unanswered? Encouraged by Jesus' words and example, the person implores heaven for restoration or relief. Yet nothing happens. Too often we chide the patient for not praying more fervently or frequently. We blame the believer's faith rather than admit the possibility that God may be at fault. The tendency is to let God off the hook when in reality it is a question of God's credibility. It would be an easy out to deny God or say that the Holy One is dead. But to be a believer is to be condemned to the struggle. "My God, my God, why . . . ?" Human experience itself raises the question of God's integrity.

The Jewish writer and philosopher Elie Wiesel has experienced the silence of God in ways that few of us can imagine. In Auschwitz, he speculated with imagination what it might have been like for Adam, fresh from the Creator's hand, to open his eyes and find himself alone in the world. Wiesel suggests that in the times of our aloneness, the elemental human question is not, "Who am I?," but, "(God,) who are you?"[9] From the beginning, it has always been a question of God's character, not God's reality.

This brings us back to the Christmas story. The gulf between fact and fancy confronts us again in a manger. This time, however, the difference is between God's fact and our fancy. Our dreams of greatness are disappointed by God's scandalous demeanor. Inebriated with much holiday cheer and stoned on the sentimentality of the season, we easily forget that Bethlehem, the City of David, remembered so glowingly by later tradition, was, in reality, the place of hated taxation. "And all went to be enrolled."

Dulled with resignation, weary to the bone, Joseph and Mary, tax collectors and prostitutes, butchers and bakers, beggar men and chiefs, all went to be enrolled in those days, plodding along the dusty, monotonous, wearisome road to Bethlehem—Bethlehem, the symbol of Roman oppression. The focus of financial hardship. The place where they were to be enrolled and taxed. The epitome of everything that was wrong with life—*Bethlehem*!

Every person has a Bethlehem. It may be a mother who, with her college degree, feels imprisoned by the dull and monotonous task of homemaking. Or the person who is told to report to the boss's office and makes the long, lonely trek down the hall, knowing what awaits him behind the closed door. Everyone has a Bethlehem.

It may be the tyranny of the past. Molded by expectations laid on by a compulsive world that confine and define us, we become what people expect—a self-fulfilling prophecy. They think we are shy, and we become shy. They think we are ineffective, and we become ineffective. They think we are worthless, and we feel worthless. Everyone has a Bethlehem.

Carl Jung, in speaking of his father, paints a picture with which many of us can identify. In his autobiography, Jung describes his father, who had graduated from seminary and entered the ministry.

> His days of glory had ended with his final examination. Thereafter he forgot his linguistic talent. As a country parson he lapsed into a sort of sentimental idealism and into reminiscences of his golden student days, continued to smoke a long student's pipe, and discovered that his marriage was not all he had imagined it to be. He did a great deal of good—far too much—and as a result was usually irritable.[10]

"We live lives of quiet desperation," said Thoreau. Life is not all we had hoped it would he. Vexed and perplexed, pressed and oppressed, we plod along the dusty road to an appointment with our fated destiny. We go to Bethlehem. Whether it be oppression or depression, boredom or hardship, all roads eventually lead, if not to Rome, then to Bethlehem. Most of us have been there. Bethlehem is that place in the world where Jesus says we will have tribulation.

Luke's Gospel offers us no illusions about the waiting world into which Jesus was thrust. He speaks disparagingly of "those days." Those days of Roman rule and oppression, those days of high taxation and hard times, those days when government corruption and the high cost of living were on everyone's mind as they conversed in the marketplace. Those days when Jewish zealots (that is, terrorists) were plotting the overthrow of the government and hijacking caravans. Those days when life was cheap and public executions—crucifixion-style—were hardly noticed.

In those days when the lame and the blind had resigned themselves to their careers of begging, like blind Bartimaeus sitting beside the dusty road going up from Jericho to Jerusalem; when tax collectors like Matthew and Zacchaeus had long since learned that the way to get ahead was to play the game and had willingly sold their souls to the system in order to make a living. In those days when frustrated fishermen like Simon and his brother, Andrew, had come to the bleak conclusion that the most life could hold for them was another day at the nets of their father's boat. In those days, a decree went out from Caesar Augustus that all the world should be enrolled and taxed and taxed and taxed.

Now it is precisely at this point that the miracle is seen. It is when we have stated the matter thusly that we are able to hear the good news. The claim Christian faith makes is that it was in *Bethlehem* in *those days*, in such a place, that the Christ was born, the new creation of God's kingdom established.

The remarkable words of the prophet come to mind. In announcing the Messianic reign he promised, "waters shall break forth in the *wilderness*, and streams in the *desert*," (Isaiah 35:6, italics added). The location of the springs of water and the streams of grace is important. They will break forth in the most unlikely place: the desert wilderness, or in Bethlehem, in "those days."

Where one would least expect it, there in Bethlehem, the new possibilities and hopes broke forth, and history was invaded by novelty that surprised the cynics. There the potency of new actions erupted, the tyranny of the past was broken, and the terror of the future gave way to hope for a new time. The dull destiny of the beggar Bartimaeus, the compromises of Matthew and Zacchaeus, and the despair of Simon and Andrew were forever altered and broken open in Bethlehem. The miracle of our faith is that Bethlehem is not remembered as a symbol of political oppression, nor the focus of financial hardship. It is no longer remembered as the epitome of all that is wrong with life. The miracle is that Bethlehem is remembered with joy because the Promise Maker is a Promise Keeper. It was in that city, in those days, and in spite of all that was wrong with the world, entrenched demons and Canaanites included, that the God of grace broke into the world with something new: new life, new beginnings, new creation.

"And his name shall be called Emmanuel," that is, God with us.

Behold the man! Whatever else we may say about Jesus, he is a man who lived in scandalous reality and tells it like it is. "In the world you have tribulation," he says. In the world there are demons. More than enough to go around. Jesus had no intention of casting them all out because it was an impossibility. So too, did Israel discover that the Canaanites were too well entrenched to ever be free of them. At worst, she would have to live with them. At best, they might become her servants. *But the miracle of grace is that we can live with the demons and the Canaanites.* We can party and sing carols in Bethlehem. We can dance and play during "those days." "In the world you have tribulation; but be of good cheer," Jesus goes on, "I have overcome the world" (John 16:33).

The fanciful myth is that we can begin living only when we have moved to the suburbs, cast out all the demons, and gotten rid of the Canaanites. To live as a human being, we are told, means we must be happy and whole. The prophets of Madison Avenue know what we need to be fully human. We do not even have to ask them. Their message is right there—all around us— inviting us to become believers. They offer us the products without which whole life is inconceivable. Human beings are people with white, sparkling teeth, who smell nice, drive sleek, shiny automobiles on their way to happy homes and prosperous jobs.

But what if in reality our jobs are deadly dull, or our marriages are on the rocks? Where is wholeness for us if our car is in the garage or the finance company has repossessed it? What if some of our teeth are missing, we sweat a lot, or have bad breath? How do we deal with fairy tales amidst the shocking realities of life? What does it mean to claim our dignity as children of the Most High in a world of barns and crosses?

The reply of Jesus is, "Take up your cross and follow me." He not only assumes that each of us will have a cross, but more remarkably, he assumes *we can bear it*. Rather than have us believe we can get rid of our crosses by earnest prayer, positive thinking, or sincere effort, Jesus, who is an expert on crosses, knows that life will assign each of us one or more to bear. The grace of God is found, not by having them miraculously disappear, but in the discovery that we can, in fact, carry them. When Jesus as God's anointed one bids us take up our cross and follow him, we need to hear his invitation, not as an onerous command to do the distasteful, but as a word of permission to live in our humanity.

What makes Jesus our Savior—the one who frees us to live joyously—is that he learned how to live in the land of the demons. Jesus lived a life tainted by scandal, yet he called it "abundant." He lived under the shadow of the cross, and yet he called it "good." He was surrounded by the blundering confusion of his disciples, and yet he was joyous. Jesus was beset by doubts and temptations, yet he was not overcome by them. He wrestled continually within himself over the meaning of his ministry and life, and yet he never became self-centered. He was betrayed and denied by his closest friends, yet he never became bitter. When we behold such a man, we know we are in the presence of the holy. We are broken to our knees and with wise men and shepherds, angels and archangels, crucified thief and Roman centurion, we confess, "Truly this was the Son of God!" (Matthew 27:54).

To call Jesus "Son of God" means essentially the same thing that Matthew does when he speaks of Jesus as "Emmanuel." What we see in him gives us a clue to what God is like. "Like Father, like son," is the way the folk proverb has it. The misgivings which we, like Job, have about God's character disappear in the presence of Jesus. When we look at him we see a God who has a vested interest in our humanity and stands with us as an unexpected ally. The veil is lifted from the featureless face of Fate. When we "Behold the man!" and take him seriously as a fellow pilgrim, we see behind him, standing in his shadow, an incredible God of grace. We find in Jesus' humanity the amazing ability to live in the land of the Canaanites with the demons and yet be neither defeated nor destroyed by them. Though we cannot do anything about the arbitrariness of life, in him we see that we do not have to. We can accept life as it is and say "Yes" to it because of the one God has made Lord. The kingdom of God consists in just this: We can live in the same land with the Canaanites and the demons.

I am moved by the courage of Debbie, the seventeen-year-old girl in Hannah Green's *I Never Promised You a Rose Garden*, who learned to live in the land of the demons. She was hospitalized in an institution for the insane. Yet her story is breathtaking as she risks leaving the security of her madness to enter again the world of reality. She recovers sufficiently to leave the hospital, although she will never be as strong as those who have not been mentally ill. Nevertheless, she leaves with a wisdom far exceeding that of those who have never lived in the land of the demons. She has learned that mental health is not the absence of depression or problems. It is the ability to *cope* with them. Mental health is not found by defeating the demons, but in choosing to do battle with them. Again and again the voices within her overpower her, and she is forced to return to the hospital for treatment. But again and again she musters her courage and returns to the world of reality. During one of her stays in the hospital, she finds that her fellow inmates resent her presence among them. Indeed, one of them is so angered that she throws a cup at her, hitting her in the head.

> [Debbie] looked again at the faces in the ward. Her presence was making them struggle with Maybes. Suddenly she realized she was . . . a living symbol of hope and failure and the terror they all felt of their own resiliency and hers, reeling punch-drunk from beating after beating, yet, at the secret bell, up again for more. She saw why she could never explain the nature of her failure to these people who so needed to understand it, and why she could never justify scraping together her face and strength to go out again . . . and again.[11]

The miracle of grace is that we go out again and again . . . and yet again to struggle with the demons and fight the Canaanites, even though we will *never* defeat them.

Faith in Jesus as Emmanuel is the conviction that our well-being is not dependent upon winning the battles in which we are engaged. Our well-being is not dependent upon driving out the Canaanites, whom we come to recognize as a permanent part of the landscape. Rather, faith is the assumption that in the battle that we are *losing*, we do not need to be anxious because we are safe in God's care and keeping. The victory of faith is not in winning the war against the enemy, the Canaanites, but in choosing to do battle with them. In choosing to do battle, we deny them their power to define and determine us.

Ad campaigns make myriads of promises about delivering the goodness of life. But life does not promise us that illusive rose garden. It does not even guarantee us justice or fairness. Life does not promise us healing, and it does not hold out the hope of deliverance from the barns or crosses, demons or Canaanites. The one thing it promises it does deliver—a variety of experiences, some good, some not so good.

The Jesus story does not convey a picture of God as a Fairy Godmother who waves her magic wand thereby changing pumpkins into royal coaches. Prayers bombarding the throne of grace stemming from this assumption result in frustration if not futility. But the story does suggest that behind the scenes stands an imaginative and creative God who offers hope for those born in barns and the ability to cope with the crosses life delivers.

The grace of God has little to do with the forgiveness of sins, as though God were shocked by our scandalous lives. Like the cleric who turns red at the telling of a dirty joke, we seem to think God is forced to look the other way out of divine embarrassment. No, the grace of God has to do with a star that shines over Bethlehem, illuminating the possibilities of life whatever the circumstances might be. Grace does not alter the circumstances of our lives, but it does change the way we see them. The power of the Jesus story lies in the permission it gives us to view the scandal of our lives in a new light—starlight. Its energy rests in the assumption that we can face the demons within, our inadequacies and our limitations, and take them seriously without being defined or determined by them. We are enabled to pick up the scattered pieces of our lives and live with them joyously.

In the Gospel of John we are given an important paradigm for living. Jesus encounters a lame beggar who complains that no one will carry him to the healing waters. He has been stuck on his pallet for thirty-eight years, begging a living, dependent on the goodwill and charity of others. Jesus simply says to him, "Take up your pallet, and walk" (John 5:8). John records that immediately the man was healed, and he took up his pallet and walked. We might amplify Jesus' words: "Stop waiting around for your ship to come in. Stop wasting your time hoping others will carry you. Take up your infirmity and start living. You have been here all your life, and all you know are these surroundings and the people who come here with crumbs for you. There is a whole wide world out there in which to live and the adventure of living in it is awaiting you. You do not need to be healed to start living. Take up your pallet and get going.''

We are cripples, yes! We are possessed by demons, yes! We live in the land of the Canaanites, yes! We have hurt and been hurt, yes! We have dung under our fingernails, yes! There is the hint of scandal about us, yes! We are sinners, yes! We are doomed to die, yes! And all of these limitations define us? No! To live by starlight is to live by the assumption that limitations, barns and crosses, weaknesses and death do not define us. To live by the light of the star is to live by the belief that if the God of grace be for us, no limitation can be against us. We may be crushed, but we are not destroyed. We may be discouraged, but we are not left in despair. Bereaved, but not reduced to hopelessness.

I may be neurotic, but my neurosis does not need to make me feel guilty. I may be ill, but my illness does not have the power to define me. I may not be able to speak or love with the ability of angels, but that disability does not deter me from speaking or loving as best I can.

To one person Jesus said, ''Take up your pallet and walk.'' But to all of us he says, ''Take up your crosses and start living.''

7

Born to Die

The problem with so many of our fantasies is that they fascinate us. We can become so successful at spinning them that we get distracted from the task of living and loving. We can become so engrossed in them that we are too busy to walk and talk with cripples, too strong to understand weakness, too successful to sympathize with failure, too busy to kneel at a manger.

Furthermore, our fantasies about power and success are nurtured by a society in which a technological mentality has convinced us that we must be in charge of things—all things. To be in control is to get results and, therefore, to no one's surprise, we have become a results-oriented society. Lyle Schaller argues that, increasingly, the trend is to sacrifice long-term benefits in favor of short-term gains.[12] Such a generalization, he contends, applies to the president of the business as well as to the president of the labor union who is negotiating a new contract. It applies to the research departments in corporations, medical schools, and governments. It applies to the policy-makers who set the payout schedules for Social Security and to the coaches recruiting athletes for the university football team.

A college student of the late 1940s who was the recipient of parental financial aid to pay tuition costs is today retired and tours the national parks in a recreational vehicle with a sign on the back that proclaims, "We're spending our children's inheritance." "Instant gratification" has become a contemporary cliché. It explains both the television commercial that advises, "You only go around once," and increased consumer spending. We want results and we want them now!

Ours is a culture where winning is the thing that matters. No one even remembers the name of the person who finished second in the hundred-meter dash in the last Olympics. The second fastest runner in the world and no one knows who it was—or cares. At a time when only the fastest, the strongest, and the most beautiful people are the ones rewarded and acclaimed; the stories about the birth of the Christ-child are easily overlooked as having nothing other than seasonal sentimental value.

But the words of an Appalachian carol come to mind:

> I wonder as I wander out under the sky
> Why Jesus, my Savior, was born for to die
> For poor ornery people like you and like I.
> I wonder as I wander out under the sky.

When the writers of the Bible looked up at the night sky about which the carol speaks, they could see some two thousand stars with the naked eye. They named some of the constellations: Orion, Cassiopeia, the Pleiades, Alpha Centaurus, the Big and Little Dipper. But, thanks to the advances of modern astronomy, we know that the Appalachian balladeer looked up at a night sky filled with so many burning suns that, had he been able to name them one a second, it would have taken him seventeen hundred years to name the stars in the Milky Way alone; a galaxy so vast that, could he have traveled at the speed of light—186,000 miles a second, it would take him ten thousand years to plumb its depths and another hundred thousand years to transverse its diameter. With the psalmist, we can exclaim, "Such knowledge is too wonderful for me; it is high, I cannot attain it" (Psalm 139:6). Yet, we are told that we wheel silently through an unmeasurable void in which ours is but one of hundreds of thousands of other known galaxies. "I wonder as I wander out under the sky. . . . "

But that which amazes the balladeer was not the canopy of stars stretched above him in all its resplendent glory. It was, rather, the question, "Why?" "Why was Jesus, my Savior, born for to die?"

All of the Gospel writers are agreed that Jesus was "born for to die." His death was no accident, nor was his living toward it an afterthought. From the time of his baptism, Jesus connected his Messianic mission with the suffering servant envisioned in the Book of Isaiah.

> Surely he has borne our griefs

and carried our sorrows;
yet we esteemed him stricken,
smitten by God, and afflicted.
But he was wounded for our transgressions,
he was bruised for our iniquities;
upon him was the chastisement that made us whole,
and with his stripes we are healed.
All we like sheep have gone astray;
we have turned every one to his own way;
and the LORD has laid on him
the iniquity of us all (Isaiah 53:4-6).

Unlike aspiring modern messiahs, such as the Ayatollah, Jesus did not gather a crowd or incite them to march on his behalf, nor call them to arms in a holy war to throw off Roman oppression. Rather, he frequently sought to avoid crowds and refused the crown of kingship. He repudiated Peter's offer of comfort when Jesus announced his impending suffering and death. He set his face to go to Jerusalem, as the Gospels put it, and continually tried to prepare his disciples for his inevitable departure. Knowingly, he antagonized the religious authorities and purposely refused the legal loopholes open to him in his trial before Pilate that would have enabled him to go free. Jesus was "born for to die."

. . . though he was in the form of God, [he] did not count equality with God a thing to be grasped, but emptied himself, taking the form of a servant, being born in the likeness of men. . . . he humbled himself and became obedient unto death, even death on a cross (Philippians 2:6-8).

The descending order from greatness to humility is significant in Paul's letter. Though Jesus was equal with God, he did not count that equality as something to be guarded. Instead he emptied himself, taking on human form. But not just any human form. It was the form of a servant—a servant who was willing to be obedient even unto death. And not just any death! Certainly not the peaceful death of old age, after a full life and surrounded by admirers. Death on a cross—the ignominious death of a common criminal, deserted and alone. Paul's conclusion is clear: Jesus had no intention of pulling rank.

The long and excited anticipation that precedes Christmas each year is rooted in a romantic myth. The fact of the matter is, Jesus was born to be a Loser! That may be a bit strong, but you decide. Look at the record closely—and objectively. For just a moment, let us set aside the rose-colored glasses of traditional dogma.

There he is, the great faith-healer, healing first this one and then that one, only to find that in a matter of months or years all those whom he helped died anyway.

There is the great teacher whose words of wisdom were never understood by his disciples or copied down, much less published. Instead, the disciples were confused. They continually asked stupid questions of him. And in the end, they deserted him because they did not understand the cross.

There is the great man of faith, hanging on the cross, crying out in his doubt, "My God, my God, why hast thou forsaken me?" (Matthew 27:46).

There is the wonder-worker who could turn water into wine, walk on the sea, or calm the storm, hanging on the cross, powerless.

And there is the long-expected king, the one who was to pull it all together, a failure at the age of thirty-three. All the dreams of his family, the expectations of his friends, the hopes of his followers, and the desires of the religious experts, were dashed because their hero was a colossal disappointment. At the risk of being sacrilegious, he was a washout.

His public relations consultants failed him miserably. We would have expected a Messiah who was God's son to be born in the religious capital of his people—Jerusalem. Perhaps even more impressive would have been a birth in the capital of the empire—Rome. But a barn? Because there was no room for him in the inn? Shabby! Where was his advance team? We might have expected some sort of fanfare for the coming of such a distinguished personage. But a baby born under questionable circumstances with the hint of scandal surrounding him is hardly the stuff of which messiahs are made. And for his life's work, we might have chosen a career in the military or politics, where a would-be messiah could have made a name for himself. But Jesus was not even—as the phrase puts it—gainfully employed. Instead, he wasted his time on the hillsides, picking flowers and talking to whoever would come out from the towns to listen to him.

And when, at last, it came time for him to die, his public relations experts could certainly have come up with something more heroic than the death of a common criminal. Add it all up, and what do you have? The man was a Loser.

What is remarkable about Jesus is not that he was born in a stable, in an insignificant community, of questionable parents, nor that he grew up to become a wandering ne'er-do-well who came to an ignominious end. What is remarkable about Jesus is that Christians have placed him at the center of their story and sing his praises!

Why?

Because of the resurrection. Had it not been for the resurrection, we would never have given the life of this man a second thought. We would not only have assumed, with the stoic or the cynic, that crucifixions and suffering are simply part of the human lot; but we would have seen that the poor fellow had two strikes against him when he came to bat. He simply struck out.

But the resurrection, like the star, causes us to look again. The resurrection is God's word spoken about the Loser. It is God's commentary on his life and death. It is as if God reaffirms the divine evaluation of Jesus at the beginning of his ministry. So now, after it is completed, "This is my beloved Son, with whom I am well pleased" (Matthew 3:17). That is to say, "I approve of the Loser. I rather like his style!" The resurrection is God's statement about a humanity that lacks the appearance of success and power—a humanity characterized instead by scandal and vulnerability. The resurrection is not an endorsement of our compulsive need to win. It is an endorsement of the humanity of Jesus, the Crucified One, the Scandalous One. Across *this* humanity, God writes, "It is good!"

Because the resurrection is God's word spoken about such humanity, it is God's word spoken about *our* humanity and the ambiguities in which we live out our lives. Weakness is as much a part of life as strength—and it is good! Suffering is as much a part of life as health—and it, too, is good! Failure is as much a part of life as success—and it is all right with God. Doubt is as much a part of life as certainty—and it has been ratified. Fear is as much a part of life as faith—and it has been approved.

Through the lifestyle of Jesus, God says to us, "I give you permission to be human. You do not have to be successful. You do not have to get your act together. You do not have to be the best parent in the world. You do not have to get that promotion. You are accepted. With all your frailty, with all your weakness, with all of the scent of scandal about you, I accept you."

The Holy One frees us from the bondage of feeling we have to be perfect. So far as the world is concerned, Jesus' cross may be a symbol of embarrassing failure, but in light of the resurrection we see it as God's permission to live and fail. The resurrection is the star that lights the cross with a meaning not derived from any assessment of this world's wisdom. We are able to declare, "If the cross is good enough for God's Son, it is good enough for me." We are freed from the tyranny of having to be winners.

I doubt that you have ever heard of Peter Strudwick. He is a marathon runner. And the reason you have never heard of him is because he has never won a race. He is a loser. When interviewed, he admitted, "I have been in forty-three marathons and I have finished last in all of them. But I did finish." What makes Peter Strudwick remarkable is that he has no feet. He runs on the stumps at the ends of his legs.

What makes Jesus remarkable is that we call him the "Son of the Most High God." By believing so, we are freed from the neurotic compulsion of trying to measure up to somebody else's success standards in order to be of worth. To believe that Jesus is the Son of God is to believe that we have been given permission to be Charlie Browns, and, despite our best intentions, to live with feet of clay; or, indeed, no feet at all. "In the world you have tribulation," said Jesus (John 16:33). In this world of production standards, social requirements, popular expectations, you will have frustrating reminders of your liabilities and limitations. "But," Jesus continues, "be of good cheer. I have overcome the world." We are free—free to be human. Free to fail, and free, ultimately, to die. "To believe in God," says Joseph Pintaure, "is to die and not be embarrassed." Jesus is that word of permission become flesh.

Is that good news? I put it before you that such an understanding of life fosters good mental health. Over the centuries people have come to realize there is a continual and unavoidable sense of conflict within themselves that cannot be ignored by covering it over with the label, "beautiful people." It is important for us, say psychiatrists, to become aware of these inner conflicts and to recognize them, not as horrible flaws, but rather as opportunities for growth. Sometimes we do grow because of these inner conflicts. Sometimes we are defeated by them. But win or lose, we have been approved.

In Arthur Miller's poignant play *Death of a Salesman*, the wife of Willie Loman talks with her son about the father with whom he has become disenchanted. She tries to explain about the man she loves.

I don't say he's a great man. Willie Loman never made a lot of money. His name was never in the paper. He's not the finest character that ever lived. But, he's a human being, and a terrible thing is happening to him. So attention must be paid. He's not to be allowed to fall into his grave like an old dog. Attention, attention must finally be paid to such a person.[13]

The birth, death, and resurrection of Jesus is God's word that attention has been paid to such a person. God may have other words for other worlds, but his word for this world is "Jesus Christ." Jesus Christ born in a barn. Jesus Christ crucified. And Jesus Christ raised from the dead. They are all part of one story and have to go together. Like the star above the stable, the resurrection is God's commentary on Christ's life and death. The stable and the cross are the symbols of life's vulnerability, its frailties, its weaknesses, its failures. And across them all, God has written, "Approved."

8

A Barn Can Be the Pits

To speak of dying amidst the joy of a birthday celebration is, to put it bluntly, in poor taste. Nevertheless, it does serve to keep us grounded in reality and reminds us that being born in a barn can be the pits! In fact, it can be downright depressing.

Christmas is, or should be, a time of joy, not sadness. Yet, despite the good news, the celebration of Jesus' birth is, oddly enough, a time of sadness for many people. Even before the needles have fallen from the trees and the ornaments packed away for another year there is, for some, a moodiness that clouds the scenes of merriment. Psychologists characterize this holiday season letdown as a time of depression. There is even an increase in the suicide rate. With all of the merrymaking, all of the holiday cheer and the anticipation of gathering with family and friends, we must wonder how Christmas could be a time of depression and sadness.

To state the matter this way is, of course, to see the problem. When Christmas is pictured in the glowing terms of yuletide advertising, we create another fantasy—the myth of the impossible dream. Like a *Good Housekeeping* ideal home, it becomes something to which all of us aspire but few of us can attain. We have idealized Christmas in all of its warmth and joy. It is portrayed as a time of sharing when the best in everyone is revealed by the smiles of happiness written on people's faces. By sad contrast, we discover that reality does not measure up to our expectations. Ours frequently turns out to be no holiday at all. We feel burdened by hectic shopping and furious preparations for family gatherings. The faster we scurry, the "behinder" we get. The lists of things to do gets longer, and the time in which to do them gets shorter. At best, we feel shortchanged. At worst, we feel there must be something wrong with us. A cartoon in the *New Yorker* catches the true spirit of the season for many: the harried housewife sitting in the squalor of her kitchen, dishes piled high in the sink, food burning in the oven, children screaming and fighting. As her husband comes in the door, returning from work, she says, "Dinner will be a little late. I've been counting my many blessings."

Over the years, we build up a cautious reservation as we are repeatedly bombarded with the "Christmas spirit." We *know* better. Nevertheless, we keep expecting it to *get* better. The Christmas hype generates sales and cynicism. But because it is very difficult to be cynical about Christmas, we turn the cynicism back on ourselves. As a result, we become depressed.

Then, too, Christmas is a time of nostalgia. It is a time of remembering Christmases past. Remembering the good times that, for whatever reason, have slipped away. Times when the children were small. Times when the folks were still alive. Times when the family gathered in the familiar living room. The present reality only serves to remind us of what we have lost. Previous Christmases found us young and hopeful. The time between Christmases seemed to drag by. We had a lifetime before us, time in which to realize dreams. Now, however, the years seem to go by like the slats in a picket fence, and the holidays come around with increasing speed. Their coming only serves to remind us of the passage of time, aging, and death—our death. Depression follows.

But whatever the psychological explanations may be for our Christmas depression, the birth of Jesus *is* an occasion of grief and tears, and Matthew's narrative tells us why.

Now when [the wise men] had departed, behold, an angel of the Lord appeared to Joseph in a dream and said, "Rise, take the child and his mother, and flee to Egypt, and remain there till I tell you; for Herod is about to search for the child, to destroy him." And he rose and took the child and his mother by night, and departed to Egypt, and remained there until the death of Herod. This was to fulfil what the Lord had spoken by the prophet, "Out of Egypt have I called my son." Then Herod, when he saw that he had been tricked by the wise men, was in a furious

rage, and he sent and killed all the male children in Bethlehem and in all that region who were two years old or
under, according to the time which he had ascertained
from the wise men. Then was fulfilled what was spoken
by the prophet Jeremiah:

> "A voice was heard in Ramah,
> wailing and loud lamentation,
> Rachel weeping for her children;
> she refused to be consoled,
> because they were no more."
> (Matthew 2:13-18)

Matthew tells us about the cruel slaying of innocent children—
all because Jesus was born. Death and grieving surround the
coming of the Messiah. The angels' admonition to the shepherds
in Luke's account, "Fear not," should have forewarned us that
there was something ominous about this baby's birth.

Jesus' mother is granted psychic foresight in what has come
to be known as Mary's Magnificat. In it she spells out some of
the ominous implications of her son's Messianic reign:

> He has shown strength with his arm,
> he has scattered the proud in the imagination of their hearts,
> he has put down the mighty from their thrones,
> and exalted those of low degree;
> he has filled the hungry with good things,
> and the rich he has sent empty away (Luke 1:51-53).

That is cause for concern if you happen to be rich, full, or
mighty. Compared to the standards by which most of the world's
population lives, all of us probably fall into one or more of those
categories. As I read Mary's prophecy, that causes me a fair
amount of anxiety. Hers is the perspective of those victimized by
the wealthy brokers of worldly power.

Nicaraguan priest Ernesto Cardenal has written of the insights
his lowly, uneducated peasant parishioners have into the meaning
of these biblical stories. As those oppressed by American colo-
nialism south of the border, they understand the Christmas story
with a clarity that often eludes us in our comfortable complacency.
One of his parishioners, for example, offers this commentary on

current events in Central America as seen through the spectacles of Jesus' birth narrative.

What we're seeing is the living story of the life of Jesus. And more Herods will come along, because whenever there's someone struggling for liberation there's someone who wants to kill him, and if they can kill him they will. How happy Samosa would have been if Ernesto and Fernando had died when they were little kids so they wouldn't be teaching all this. It's perfectly clear that the business of Herod and Christ, we have it right here.[14]

It is perfectly clear to these students of the Bible, if not to us, that Jesus was a subversive and that the telling of his story has revolutionary implications for our hemisphere.

Certainly it was made clear to Mary and Joseph, the wee tyke's loving and devoted parents. They had to pay a heavy price for the coming of Christ into their lives. Practically overnight, they became an endangered species, and all because of this baby born to them. Quite literally, they had to run for their lives. Matthew says the celebration had hardly begun when they were told they would have to live as aliens in a foreign land *because* of their son! Forced into the inconvenience and disruption of exiled living, away from home and thrown upon the mercy of strangers in Egypt, Mary and Joseph, no doubt, had plenty of time to reflect upon their loneliness, if indeed, they were not too depressed to do so. This bouncing baby boy in their midst was a danger to life and limb. And why? Because the power of Herod was threatened. He sensed in this divine visitation something that would challenge his law and order, alter the priorities of his people, and render relative his authority. So Mary and Joseph had to pay the penalty. Their lives were never the same again.

But that is only the beginning of the misery. All of the parents in and around Bethlehem had to pay a price for the coming of the Christ. As Matthew tells the story, Herod was so threatened and enraged that he began a systematic liquidation of all the male children two years of age and under. He was taking no chances. Imagine the weeping! Picture the sorrow! The scene is reminiscent of those recorded by newsmen during the war in Vietnam, where whole villages of innocent women and children got caught in the cross fire between the two warring armies and were utterly wiped out. Talk about Christmas depression! Is granting God's birthday wish—the entry of the Holy One into the arena of human affairs—worth such a price?

We must wonder if any page of history is worth writing with the blood of six million Jews. Is the defense of any principle worth the cost of a nuclear holocaust that renders Spaceship Earth uninhabitable except for cockroaches? Is the gift of divine grace worth the cost of so many innocent children's lives?

And the slaughter, of course, raises the equally depressing question: Who made Herod's weapons? Who sold him the swords? Without them his soldiers could not have carried out their murderous orders. Whoever it was, they too, must share in the responsibility of innocent death. They, too, have blood on their hands.

No doubt the shareholders of the German chemical company that produced the Zyclon gas Hitler used as the "final solution to the Jewish problem" rejoiced at the increased profits reported at their annual meeting. But they also stand responsible before the jury of the dead.

An investment newsletter to which I subscribe offered a recommendation for a stock that it believed would be a good buy. The report read,

> Clabir corporation listed on the American Stock exchange is an intriguing military spending and asset play, and is recommended for purchase. Clabir's primary interest is its 67% owned general defense subsidiary that is the US Army's primary supplier of live and training tank projectiles and other tank ordinance. The Army plans to increase its tank weaponry expenditure from $150 million to $500 million annually . . . so Clabir should experience significant earnings gains in the years ahead.

There is money to be made by producing and selling arms to Herod! The disclosures of Colonel Oliver North during the Congressional investigation of the Iranian-Contra scandal made that abundantly clear.

Nor are swords and tank projectiles the only means by which money is killing innocent children. For years the World Council of Churches called for a boycott of Nestle's food products because their marketing of infant formula resulted in the starvation of babies. Nestle promoted the product in the third world nations while knowing full well that poverty-stricken people frequently do not have the technological means to sterilize bottles or the knowledge to take the necessary precautions to prevent disease. Not knowing how to read directions, unsuspecting mothers mixed the infant formula with contaminated water, sometimes diluting it in an attempt to stretch the household budget. The result was colored water, with little or no nutritional value. But the third world is a lucrative market. As a consequence of Nestle's promotional efforts, profits rose, breast-feeding declined, and malnutrition increased.

Even the best of intentions can result in the deaths of innocent children when national policy is misguided or naive. Whatever other differences Secretary of State Haig and Secretary of Defense Weinberger may have had in the early years of the Reagan administration, they were agreed on one thing: They saw food as a military weapon. As a result, it was thought that a wheat embargo would force the Polish government to adopt a more lenient stance regarding the human rights of its citizens. Apparently, it was believed by high officials in the administration that if there was a food shortage in Poland, it would be the soldiers and politicians who would go hungry. Whatever the merits of such a foreign policy, the administration's faith in human nature is remarkable. I suspect a more realistic appraisal of the priorities of people with power is that civilians would be among the first to suffer and, certainly, children. The end result would likely be the intentional starvation of innocent victims.

To have our consciences sensitized is to disrupt the complacent coziness that allows us to sleep soundly on Christmas Eve with visions of sugarplums dancing in our heads. When we hear the story of the baby born in a barn—the whole story—we become aware of all those innocent children. We begin to sense our responsibility for their deaths in the interconnectedness of our world. Christmas is a time of depression because the coming of Christ makes us aware of the world around us and the precious people who live—and die—in it.

What, then, is the good news?

Perhaps this. All of the weeping, all of the despair, all of the sorrow, all of the suffering—all of it was anticipated by the Most High. None of it caught the Holy One by surprise. This is not a perfect world nor does it have to be in order for God to be Emmanuel—God with us. God did not wait until the world cleaned up its act before the Holy One decided to honor us with a visit. All of the mourning and despair did not deter God from touching down on this planet. Matthew recalls that it was the Old Testament prophet who saw clearly God's determination and that it would be out of Egyptian exile that God would have to call the child. The exile was foreseen. The persecution of innocent children did not catch God unaware. Before Jesus was born, the prophet Jeremiah foretold the weeping and lamentation for the slaughter of the innocent children. It was not, therefore, news to God.

The Good News is that Jesus is called Emmanuel—God with us. His coming among us is not *dependent* on our Christmas cheer, or prosperity, or family gatherings. Nor is Emmanuel *prevented* from being present with us because of illness, suffering, and death, much less our feelings of unworthiness, guilt, or despair.

Sometimes people will ask me as a clergyperson to pray for them because they do not "feel close to God," as though God's presence with us were dependent upon our endocrine glands. Feelings? What have feelings to do with prayer? What have feelings to do with the closeness of Emmanuel?

The significance of the Christmas story is not the sentimentality in which it has become mired but the perspective on life which it offers. We all enjoy the so-called "Christmas spirit." We agree that the world would be a better place if only we could maintain its emotional high year-round.

But Ebenezer Scrooge helps keep things in perspective. His "Bah! Humbug!" serves as a needed corrective to our merry-making. Scrooge's cynicism brings us up short by reminding us that, if Christmas is only an emotional jag, it is not worth all of the attention that we Christians give to it.

The Gospel writers tell the Christmas story in a straightforward manner. It lacks the emotional hype and background detail that a modern motion picture director would give it. But the succinct way in which they tell the story makes it clear that whether we have chills running up and down our spine or find ourselves tingling with emotion is really irrelevant. Our subjective response is not the issue. Their point is: At a time and place in history, the awaited promise was kept. A divine communique was delivered to earth in the person of Jesus of Nazareth that can alter the way we view life. Luke even goes so far as to tell us that the birth of Jesus occurred during the days of Caesar Augustus, at the time of his first enrollment when Quirinius was governor of Syria. "The Word," as John says, "became flesh and dwelt among us, full of grace and truth; we have beheld his glory . . ." (John 1:14). Not in theory, but in historical fact.

I take it, therefore, that the good news lies beyond our emotional response to it. Before we were born, before we had any say in the matter, and most certainly before we had any feelings about it one way or the other, the Holy One visited this planet.

Whether we feel good or not, depressed or joyous, God has decided to join us. Whether we feel close to God or not has nothing to do with the fact that at a point in time, at a particular place on this earth, Emmanuel was born—born amidst the weeping and fears of nameless common folk. The birth of Jesus makes it clear, for those who have eyes to see and ears to hear: This totally mundane world of injustice and treachery has been favored with the divine presence.

The message of Christmas is that the Holy One has vowed to be with us. "The light shines in the darkness, and the darkness has not overcome it" (John 1:5). Not Herod and his vicious vendetta, not the loneliness of exile, not the suffering of innocent children or the cries of anguished parents—none of it deterred God from coming into this world. Our feelings of guilt and despair cannot prevent God from coming into our lives either. In Jesus we have God's guarantee to be Emmanuel.

So it was that the divine emissaries announced in the night: Fear not—you who are afraid, you who are guilty, you who are responsible and must be held accountable, you who are bowed low with depression—fear not, for behold, though you can never understand it and certainly are not worthy of it, behold, I tell you good news of a great joy. "For to you is born this day in the City of David a Savior, who is Christ the Lord."

9

Impossible Humanity

There is no story in the Christmas collection that is better known and less understood than Luke's story concerning the "virgin birth" of Jesus. Luke sets the scene for us with a persuasive Gabriel making his pitch to an understandably startled, but preciously naive Mary. She is to bear a divine son. That much is clear. But she wonders,

> "How shall this be, since I have no husband?" And the angel said to her,
> "The Holy Spirit will come upon you,
> and the power of the Most High will overshadow you;
> therefore the child to be born will be called holy,
> the Son of God.
> For with God nothing will be impossible" (Luke 1:34-35, 37).

Unfortunately, Luke's story has suffered at the hands of theological hard hats, who have set it in dogmatic concrete. Sadly, many Christians have made the virgin birth an article of faith. Unless you believe in it, along with belief in the literal physical resurrection of Jesus, you do not qualify for the team. It is unfortunate, not only because a literal understanding of the story requires suspension of the intellect—substituting instead belief in a miracle—but, more importantly, because it misses the point of the story itself.

Luke's account is not written to make a biological assertion about Jesus. He is not concerned about telling us how the conception of Jesus took place—a baby conceived in a woman's womb without benefit of male sperm.

That is indeed fortunate for us as thinking Christians because our first considered response is one of skepticism. "Biologically," we say, "it is impossible." Our doubts are not helped by the well-meaning attempts of some literalists who have gone to great lengths trying to convince us that a virgin birth is possible. They refer to *parthenogenesis* and point to the fact that spontaneous conception is known to occur among bees. It can even take place in female rabbits if their temperature is lowered far enough. The problem, of course, is that without male chromosomes all of the offspring resulting from spontaneous conception can only turn out to be females.

But even granting that miraculously parthenogenesis could result in the production of a male child, we are left with a biological curiosity. If the bottom line of Luke's account is to be taken as biological fact, Jesus becomes a medical freak. And that does not, it must be noted, make him the Son of God! To be born of a virgin no more makes Jesus the Son of God than it would if he had been born with three heads. It simply makes him a carnival curiosity. Even if we take the story literally, therefore, we still have to make the classic leap of faith about who Jesus was and is. There is no way we can escape the risk of making some assumption about him, no way we can escape living by starlight.

But, returning to the story: Luke does not tell it in order to make a a biological assertion about the origin of Jesus. Rather, he seeks to make a *theological* point. Luke calls us to see the impossibility of this man's *humanity*.

The Gospels do not attempt to idealize Jesus by portraying his angelic qualities. This is a remarkable fact, since they obviously wanted to proclaim the good news of Jesus' significance and gain a hearing among their readers for their message. What they do offer is a portrait of an amazing human being with all his strengths and frailties. As we have seen, no attempt is made to hide the scandal of his humanity. No mention is made of a halo about Jesus' head. Instead, the Gospels speak of his frustration during the final weeks of his life. He was so frustrated and irritable, in fact, that the disciples were afraid to ask him any more questions (Mark 9:32). They speak of his sweat as he prayed in Gethsemane (Luke 22:39-46). And with no special insight into the future, other than a shrewd analysis of how things were going, Jesus apparently found the thought of his death threatening and repulsive. With the ears of imagination we can hear him argue about obedience to what he believed to be his Father's will for him.

> Let this cup pass from me. I don't want to die! I can't see any point in it. My psychiatrist thinks I am suffering from a martyr complex. When I try to tell her that the cross is your will, she just looks at me and shakes her head. "Death wish," she mumbles. Besides, there are so many other ways to make the Kingdom known. I thought about them in the wilderness several years ago. Any one of them is more reasonable than this absurd death-on-a-cross idea. A few more miracles to convince the crowds. A little more time to educate the disciples. If they are to carry the message, it's obvious they need more time. They're too confused. Surely, there's no hurry. Maybe next month or next year if you still feel that dying is necessary. But not now! It doesn't fit.

I, for one, can identify with that kind of humanity. I expect most of us know the pull between what we feel we *ought* to do, and what we *want* to do. It is just this humanity which not only gets my attention but bothers me. His humanity is different from mine. He says, "Nevertheless, not my will, but thine, be done" (Luke 22:42). He is consistently obedient to the "oughtness" in his life in a way that I am not. He is free to respond to God's will in a way that I am not free. The Gospel stories portray a person who constantly reminds me of the fact that I am not that man! And the more I try to be, the more obvious does the difference become.

Here is the real miracle of the man: his *impossible humanity*. He is human in a way in which we are not. Is this not his real uniqueness? Is this not the functional meaning of the New Testament's claim that Jesus is the "Son of God?" Not that he had holy genes or divine blood coursing through his veins, whatever that means. But that in a time when "God" was the explanation for everything that could be explained in no other way, these writers wanted to shout from the roof tops that here was a person of no human explanation; a person of no other explanation than "God!" They could not account for this man's humanity by adding up male sperm and female egg—Joseph plus Mary. Normal explanations could not account for this amazing person. So the story was written to point up the miraculous humanity of Jesus. When we allow the emphasis of the story to be placed on the *divinity* of Christ, he is effectively removed from the scene in which we must live out our lives. The story, then, becomes simply a wonder story—a miraculous display of divine power. A virgin conceives. Amazing! No wonder Jesus was more powerful than a locomotive, able to leap tall buildings in a single bound, and could walk on water faster than a speeding bullet. It goes with the territory.

Not only are we unimpressed, but Jesus takes his place in the lineup alongside all of the other comic book heroes. Stressing the divinity of Jesus trivializes his birth narratives, not to mention those of his life, death, and resurrection. As a result, Christmas and Easter have become cultural rituals—times for families to gather, go to church, and celebrate traditions. They have become holidays in our society, featuring Santa Claus and Easter bunnies and offering opportunity for economic interests to increase their profits. But they are almost devoid of any serious reflection about their theological significance.

That the traditional interpretation of Jesus as Son of God no longer has the power to hold the attention of many people is seen in how it has become a sentimental tale dramatized in church Christmas pageants by folks wearing bathrobes. It has lost its theological cutting edge. As Dietrich Bonhoeffer noted, we have "come of age." Ours is a *secular* world in which any assumptions about God have themselves become problematic.

Secularism means that we can make sense of life without any reference to the supernatural whatsoever. We assume that it is human ingenuity, government, or industry that will solve the problems of the world. Our destiny is in our hands—or at least, someone's hands. If not ours, then big government's or big business' hands. But not God's. When the chemistry professor questions the class about the bubbling reaction in a test tube, students receive no credit for saying, "God makes it happen." In an earlier time such a reply might have earned an "A," but in today's world it draws a laugh of derision except in the most conservative educational circles. In a secular world, molecular reaction is the cause and the correct answer. "God" is irrelevant.

Even granting that behind the molecular response stands a

First Cause that we can call "God," and that the splendors of space and the intricacy of an atom testify to the Creator's presence, the question still remains: Does such a God make any difference at the point where we live our lives? It seems we do business, not with a remote First Cause, but with immediate, secondary causes. We do not come to the throne of grace with requests for our daily bread. We go to the supermarket and buy our manna with cash or check in hand. We can, in fact, get along quite well without the word "God" in our vocabularies.

This is a crucial difference between our secular world and that earlier time when the orthodoxies of the church were fashioned. Those formulations began with a surefire winner: God. Nearly everybody with an ounce of sense believed in God. Supernatural forces—demons and devils, angels and God—all were assumed to be part of the scheme of things. These forces explained everything from the weather to illness and health. Jesus was therefore marketable as the "Son of God."

But in a world where God's relevancy becomes more and more problematic, trying to interpret Jesus as the Son of God in the traditional way is not going to ensure the success of the enterprise. As long as we begin with "God" and then move to Jesus as God's Son, thereby putting the emphasis on his divinity, we offer faith assumptions that are too easily dismissed by a secular world.

Moreover, a divine Christ can never really intersect the concerns of our scandalous lives. Jesus may have performed his miracles, died forgiving his enemies, and been raised from the dead; but after all, what else would you expect from a divine being? We can applaud the exploits of the gods, but in actual fact they have little to say to us as mere mortals.

Rather, therefore, than putting the spotlight on Jesus as the Son of God, let us remove him from the glare of the traditional understanding and look again at him in the soft light of the star. If we permit the star to illuminate the scenes, we see them in a different light. We see the *impossible humanity* of Jesus as the miracle.

The earliest emphasis was on the humanity of Jesus, not his divinity. The title "Son of God" originated with the early church. It is one of the ways first-century believers spoke of Jesus. But by no means the only way. In that early time, Christian thinkers used a variety of titles in their attempts to understand and communicate his significance. All of them enjoyed some popularity with various segments of the Christian community: "Son of God," "Teacher," "Lord," "King," "Christ" or "Messiah," "Prophet," "Counselor," "Comforter," and "Son of Man," to name only a few.

Jesus seems to have referred to himself as, "The Son of Man." We can only guess at his reasons for doing so. Perhaps he had in mind the messianic figure spoken of in the Old Testament Book of Daniel, or it could have been Ezekiel's concept of the representative human being. We simply do not know. We do know that Mark, the author of the first Gospel to be written, favored the "Son of Man" as his designation for Jesus. Whatever their reasons, ours is a more practical one. When we speak of Jesus in this way we uncover a rich vein of ore in the theological gold mine abandoned by both the church and the secular world.

To think of Jesus as the Son of Man is to see the title "Son of God" in a new light. By focusing on the humanity of Jesus we find that the word "God" must be reintroduced into the discussion—not because Jesus is born of a virgin, but because he is himself the miracle. We see that his amazing humanity is only a possibility of the Most High. If we begin with the humanity of Jesus rather than his divinity, we may yet be able to work our way back to meaningful God language in this secular age. Such a way of understanding the divinity of Jesus may have great relevance because God can then be seen, not as a remote Creator or First Cause of the world "out there," but as the source of Jesus' humanity. And ours!

Furthermore, to place the emphasis on the humanity of Jesus enables us to identify with him. He is one of us. He becomes our Savior in a new and significant way because he speaks our language. As Savior, he gives us permission to live our scandalously human lives as though . . . they have been approved by God. Approved, that is! Not simply forgiven. With the Son of Man as our Savior, it is no longer necessary for God to forgive our human shortcomings as if excusing our very existence were required.

The problem I have with the traditional sin/forgiveness theology is that while God may forgive me and call me righteous, God does so *in spite of* who I am. The reality of my humanity is: I am a sinner. God must accept me in spite of myself, but certainly not because of who I am. My being, therefore, is denied at the very center of my existence. In my totality, I stand before God as both good and bad. But in the presence of One who is the Ground of all Being, part of my being is rejected. God grants me a pardon and thereby calls me righteous, but God and I both know that I am not righteous. I am a sinner. I am a mixture of wheat and tares. Consequently, I end up feeling like a forgiven sinner. Instead of feeling free, I feel guilty. I may stand acquitted before the jury, but before them I feel awkward and depressed. For I know I am, in myself, unacceptable in the eyes of the Judge.

Fortunately, both Jesus and God assume we are sinners. They know, even if we do not, that sin is a fact of human existence like the color of our hair or the set of our jaws. The only possible ethical imperative, therefore, is to "sin to the glory of God," to use Luther's pungent phrase. The alternative is to curl up in some womblike corner and choose not to live at all. Our churchly confessions of sin ought not be made in order to remove it but rather to affirm our being courageously before the throne of grace. If God is to love us at all, it cannot be in spite of our sin, as if it were foreign to our true nature and could be overlooked by divine benevolence. No! If God is to love us, it must be as bon-afide sinners.

When we allow the scandalous humanity of Jesus to define his function as Savior, we are offered something more than a passport through heaven's gates. We are given a boon for living our less than perfect lives—here, in this world.

The story, then, that Luke tells about a virgin birth is a story of miracle life, and he hangs a star above it that invites us to view our own lives in the same light and be amazed! To take the story seriously as a theological statement about the humanity of Jesus rather than a biological explanation of his divinity is to see that God is not to be sought in the spectacular miracles about which religion likes to speak. Indeed, to listen to the claims made by some radio and television evangelists about sudden healings, powerful deliverances, and instantaneous conversions is to derive the distinct impression that talk becomes brag. But Luke's account directs our attention to the almost overlooked miracle of our own lives.

Sometimes the secular world is more aware of the incandescence of ordinary life than we believers. A television commercial for a well-known beer takes some of the most common, mundane moments of life and transforms them into extraordinary times of refreshment with a bottle of its beverage: the end of a working day for a salesperson who comes home and there finds warmth and acceptance—and a beer; the gathering of colleagues in the local tavern for a beer and sharing the frustrations and drudgery of oyster fishing.

While I am certainly not intending to make a pitch for anyone's product, it seems to me that these commercials have done what the star in Luke's story does—turn our attention to these overlooked episodes of ordinary existence where God meets us; episodes that are, in fact, quite extraordinary when the element of grace is added. By that are, in fact, quite extraordinary when the element of grace is added. By standing with Luke we see the miraculous gift of our lives bathed in the same light as that of Jesus. We discover the grace-full-ness of our own existence. If his story touches us, we discover the transforming effect of the star. Nothing in our scandalously ordinary lives is the same, and we see our lives, along with that of Jesus, as touched by grace.

10

Once in a Lifetime

And in that region there were shepherds out in the field, keeping watch over their flock by night. And an angel of the Lord appeared to them, and the glory of the Lord shone around them, and they were filled with fear. And the angel said to them, "Be not afraid; for behold, I bring you good news of a great joy which will come to all the people; for to you is born this day in the city of David a Savior, who is Christ the Lord. And this will be a sign for you: you will find a babe wrapped in swaddling cloths and lying in a manger." And suddenly there was with the angel a multitude of the heavenly host praising God and saying,

"Glory to God in the highest,
and on earth peace among men with whom he is pleased!"
(Luke 2:8-14)

Luke's description of the angelic announcement makes it clear that the press conference was not greeted with rave reviews. The good news of life created apprehension in the audience. The shepherds regarded the Son of Man's arrival with a sense of foreboding: "An angel of the Lord appeared to them, . . . and they were filled with fear." But the undaunted angel departed from the prepared statement to reassure them, "Be not afraid; for behold, I bring you good news of a great joy which will come to all the people. . . . "

Their reaction is understandable because we are included in "all the people" being addressed. And we spend a good deal of time doing just what the shepherds did—being afraid. Like them, we fear the good news of Life. By fear I do not mean the kind that causes us to lock doors or look under the bed. I am referring to the kind of fear that causes us, as human beings, to consume tons of tranquilizers, suffer from ulcers, and die of heart attacks. I am talking about the fear of living, of not measuring up to the expectations we allow others to lay on us. The fear that we are not good enough. The fear that the job is bigger than our performance capability. The fear that we are letting others down by not being all they expect of us.

Probably there are no words that control human behavior more than, "What will others think?" We are intimidated by them time and again. Many of us never experience the vast dimensions of our own lives or explore the potential of our capabilities because we are afraid. We are afraid that we are incompetent. We are afraid of ridicule. We are afraid to risk living for fear of what others might think if we fail—others whom we regard as more of an authority on our lives than we are.

In Nikos Kazantzakis' novel, the English friend of *Zorba the Greek* is reminded over and over of the adventurous life that has eluded him. He is both intrigued and threatened by Zorba's dances in the middle of the night. They lure him to leave the safe havens of prudence and custom in order to depart on great voyages to another world. Yet, he is unable to respond. He sits there motionless and shivering. He is ashamed. He has felt this shame before, whenever he caught himself not daring to do what supreme recklessness, the essence of life, called him to do. Yet never did he feel more ashamed than in the presence of Zorba.

Ashamed and fearful! Two sides of the same coin. And both caused when we stand in the presence of awesome humanity. "And [the shepherds] were filled with fear." I suspect many of us have felt that way. We sit before life, shivering, afraid to risk the dance for fear we will make fools of ourselves. Life intimidates us.

It is to us, therefore, that the angels speak. "Be not afraid; for behold, I bring you good news of a great joy which will come to all the people." We, the people! We stand in the presence of One who honors human life, has consecrated it as the vehicle for divine revelation, and calls us to rejoice in the miracle of our own lives. The word, both spoken by the angel and embodied in Jesus, says in effect, "Live!"

Karl Barth believed that the word of God always addresses us with a word of permission. The word conveys a life-giving power. The power in the Christmas and Easter message is that neither life nor death is able to diminish us, because God is in both as a hand is in a glove. The good news is that we do not need to be afraid of accepting our lives as precious gifts from the hand of God. No matter how scandalous or distasteful circumstances may seem, life, and what it has to offer us, cannot diminish the dignity of our humanity. Its value has been established by God in Christ.

My high school band director was frequently greeted with silence when he gave the downbeat. No sound at all! As fledgling musicians, we were unsure of ourselves, each of us hesitating, waiting for someone else to risk the first note. In exasperation the director threw down his baton—like a gauntlet thrown down in challenge—and demanded, "I'd rather have a good, big, loud mistake than no sound at all." His word of permission moved us to oblige him with multitudes of mistakes, but in between there was some recognizable music. In the case of our band, it seemed to be a case of not being able to have the one without the other.

So with life.

My two daughters, Christie and Susan, took piano lessons in their youth. As they progressed to increasingly more difficult compositions, they made mistakes and hit sour notes, but the beauty of their music increased as well. The aim of piano instruction, I take it, is to enable the student to play ever more difficult, complex, and beautiful pieces of music, rather than simply concentrate on removing the mistakes from the familiar ones that can be played with ease. Making mistakes was a necessary part of my daughters' growing ability to play beautiful music. So with our lives. Risking mistakes is a necessary part of our increasing capacity to embrace life's invitation to dance.

This is the good news of the Jesus story. However, it is not simply a general invitation to dance. It is extremely specific. As we noted in the last chapter, the relevance of the Christmas story for us is its invitation to consider, on the one hand, the miracle of Jesus' humanity and, on the other, the miracle of our own. I use the term "invitation" advisedly because the story does not push us; it does not demand of us; it only nudges us in the direction of amazement. It invites us to look at our own birth—the fact of it and the unique opportunity it provides us for living. This sense of uniqueness, when grasped by our imagination, causes us to see the remarkable opportunity that has been given each of us to live a miracle.

Consider, if you will, the miracle of my birth and, in the process, the miracle of your own. At a point in time, one egg out of thousands of others in my mother's body ripened and began its journey of destiny into her waiting womb. There it was doomed to die unless within a period of twenty-four hours it was fertilized. But it did not die. That particular egg survived because it was fertilized by a sperm cell, one of over five hundred million other possibilities from my father's body. Most of its companions died in the process of trying to reach my mother's egg, were killed by acids in her body, went in the wrong direction, or just grew tired and gave up. Had any other sperm cell of my father reached that egg, I would not have been. Someone else would have been, but not me! It was a one-in-500-million long shot. But that particular sperm cell made it, and my conception took place!

Yet this is only the beginning of the miracle story. When that particular egg in my mother's body ripened, half of its forty-six chromosomes were sloughed off. The half that remained and the half that were discarded were determined purely by chance. As if some providential bookmaker were setting the odds at one chance in eight million, the chromosomes happened to split the way they did. Had they divided in any other way, I would not be who I am. I would be different.

Meanwhile, what was taking place in the egg cell of my mother was happening in that one sperm cell of my father. The chromosomes were drawing straws in another lottery with the odds of winning set at one in eight million. Again, if the split had taken place in any one of those millions of other combinations, I would be a different person. When you begin to calculate the odds of my being, they are astronomical.

Life has not only given me permission to live; it has extended me an infinitely rare invitation to do so. There has not been another person like me in the history of the human race. There is no other person in the world like me, and there never will be another person like me. When I think of how close I came to not being here at all, I shudder. More to the point, I am humbled with gratitude.

Kurt Vonnegut has written some superb lines that catch the delight:

God made mud . . .
God got lonesome . . .
So God said to some mud, "Sit up! . . .
See all I've made," said God, "the hills,
the sea, the sky, the stars." . . .
And I was some of the mud that got to sit up
and look around . . .
"Lucky me, lucky mud."[15]

I still remember with considerable pain the embarrassment of grade-school recess. We would choose up sides to play ball. I was not very good, and I would stand there feeling awkward and inadequate. Intimidated and frightened, I wished that recess were over. But then I heard my name called: Robert!" How beautiful it sounded to me! Somebody wanted me on his team. And so I played. Poorly, perhaps, but I played, because I had been called. My name had been sounded.

The gospel is the good news that life has sounded our name. We are called to life as Robert or Ralph, as Jane or Joyce, as Mary or Mark. We are called to live out the miracle of our uniqueness. Not to be copies of someone else. Not to try and be what others think we should be, but to be fully ourselves.

Very risky business indeed, since there are no blueprints to follow. We are each one of a kind. We are not called to be little imitations of Jesus or anyone else. Just ourselves. We cannot live by the guide, "What would Jesus do?" Jesus does not have the answer for us. That is between us and our Creator, just as it was for him. Furthermore, the attempt to be like Jesus in the name of piety is to successfully do away with our own selfhood. Never mind that we have no idea what Jesus would do in the complex interrelationships of today's industrial society. Never mind that the question is simplistic. The fact is that Jesus never required his disciples to become like him. He loved and honored their uniqueness. He cherished their diversity. He did not try to iron out their idiosyncrasies. He saw them as gifts.

Peter had a spitfire temper and the impetuosity of a schoolboy. A psychiatrist would have said, "That's going to be a problem for a church leader. Better get some counseling or not enter the ministry." But Jesus looked at his neurosis and said, "I can build a church on it."

In his book *Modern Man in Search of a Soul*, Carl Jung observed in 1933 that it is no easy matter to live a life modeled on Christ, but it is unspeakably more difficult to live one's own life as truly as Christ lived his.[16] The question for Christians living today is not, "What would Jesus do?," for he has left us here, not to live his life, but our own. That is far more difficult. No one can do my living for me, or dying either, for that matter. God has not given my life to you, nor your life to someone else. No one but you will be held accountable for it. The quality of my life cannot be measured by some external standard. It can only be measured by the potential of *my* being. I am to be who *I* am. God is calling me to be me, and no one else.

In the legend of King Arthur and the Knights of the Round Table, a vision of the holy grail comes to Sir Gawain. He vows to set off in search of it the very next day. All the other Knights of the Round Table vow that they, too, will go in search of the sacred chalice. But they will not journey together. As dawn breaks the following morning, each of the knights enters the forest—alone—where he perceives it to be the darkest and the thickest. None of the knights follow a pathway. To do so would be to go where someone else had already searched.

Like the search for the holy grail, to find ourselves is not something we can do by walking someone else's path. No one can show us the way. It is rather a search we carry on by ourselves. It is the internal search of the possibility of our own becoming. Being "good" or doing the "right" thing are guides to living that assume an external and authoritative blueprint by which to pattern our lives. But none exists. We have been left here to work out our own wholeness, to paraphrase the apostle Paul, in fear and trembling (cf. Philippians 2:12).

Feelings of inadequacy and guilt come easily when we compare ourselves to some external standard of conduct or achievement. The forces of religion frequently play on them and use their leverage to gain conformity. But it is a sick guilt, and it immobilizes us. It is what MacLeish calls "the sick scent of dung under our fingernails."

Healthy guilt comes from our failure to discover the miracle of our own unique life. I cannot imagine anything more horrible than coming to the end of life with the realization that William Robert McClelland had not lived it to the fullest, that he had not drunk the cup of each moment to the bottom. The cup that life hands me to drink is, of course, different from the one that it hands you. That is another reason why living by comparing one life with another is futile. I cannot drink your cup, but I can drink mine. Indeed, no one can do it for me. True guilt, healthy guilt, motivates us rather than incapacitates us. It comes, not from comparing cups, but from the realization that we have failed to drink the cup that is ours.

Jesus tried to dislodge from the minds of his followers the concept of living by comparison, which produces unhealthy guilt. He did so by referring to the Law: the external norm of moral perfection.

> "If you would enter life," [Jesus said], "keep the commandments." [A young man] said to him, "Which?" And Jesus said, "You shall not kill, You shall not commit adultery, You shall not steal, You shall not bear false witness, Honor your father and mother, and, You shall love your neighbor as yourself." The young man said to him, "All these I have observed; what do I still lack?" Jesus said to him, "If you would be perfect, go, sell what you possess and give to the poor, and you will have treasure in heaven; and come, follow me." When the young man heard this he went away sorrowful; for he had great possessions (Matthew 19:17-22).

The young man in the story asks, "What must I do to have eternal life?" It is a bad question because he is assuming that salvation is to do something rather than to be someone. As his response to Jesus indicates, he believes salvation is found by fulfilling perfectly the obligations of God's law. He is, therefore, on a different wavelength than Jesus. But Jesus answers his bad question with an obviously absurd answer designed to display the impossibility of ever being saved, given the young man's premise. Jesus says, in effect, "If you're going to go that route, that is, if you want to be perfect, keep all of the commandments."

We must remember that Jesus had earlier redefined all of the commandments in such a way that it was obvious no one could keep them (cf. Matthew 5:21-30). To commit adultery, for example, is not to go to bed with someone else's spouse but rather to *think* about it. To kill is not only to commit the act of murder but to be *angry* with the other person. (All those who can claim innocence by such definitions may come to the front of the class.) Nevertheless, the young man claims that he has kept all of the commandments. He thinks he is well on his way to perfection and commendation. But Jesus, with a twinkle in his eyes, decides to teach him a lesson and says, "If you really want to be perfect, try this commandment on for size. Go and sell all that you have and give it to the poor, and come, follow me."

The young man went away sorrowful because he discovered what maturity teaches: None of us is perfect. That route is a dead end. Our seeking of it is an exercise in futility and frustration. This young man's fantasy was that he thought he could comply with the divine requirements for perfection. In reality, he found he could not part with his money and was thus disillusioned. We all fall short at some point. That is what Jesus wanted him—and us—to discover.

So we are left with the scandal of our weakness and are confronted, once again, with the awkwardness and risk of being ourselves. These words by Lowell Streiker describe both the agony and the ecstasy of our dilemma.

> Maturity or self-realization requires that I become aware of the unique, irreplaceable potentialities of my existence as a person and that I accept responsibility for actualizing them. Self-realization is a painful, gradual process marked by many reversals, defeats, and disappointments. Since what I was meant to be is different from what anyone else was meant to be, no formula, maxim, generalization, or dogma can distinguish for me between the real and the apparently real. Within all the circumstances which condition my existence, I must stumble along my path, discovering and actualizing the real "I."[17]

No excuses can cover up our failure to be ourselves. There is only one of you and one of me. If we blow it, no one else can do it for us. The story of Zusya makes the point. When getting old and nearing death, Zusya, the Rebbe of Annitol, said to his disciples, "After I die and go to the heavenly courts to be judged, God will not say to me, 'Zusya, why weren't you Moses?' Instead, the Creator will say to me, 'Zusya, you could have at least been Zusya, so why weren't you?'"

A television commercial calls attention to the fact that we only go around once. Life can be, and often is, awkward and even painful, but we only have one crack at it. One chance to experience all of the ups and downs, the joys and the sorrows, that constitute our special adventure. We become aware of the privilege of living, the whole of it, the good as well as the bad. In a *Peanuts* cartoon Lucy talks to the dog Snoopy: "You know there are times when you really bug me." And then she thinks, "But I also admit there are times when I feel like giving you a hug." So she hugs Snoopy. He stands there with that infectious grin on his face and says, "That's the way I am, buggable and huggable."

Life, like Snoopy, is buggable and huggable, but we become attached to it. Considering the alternative, it is nice to have around. We instinctively resent not living. We resent our death. We have been around long enough to know that we want the whole loaf. We see life as too short to meet all of the strangers, experience all of the pleasures, love all the lovable people, visit all of the world's cultures, see all of the waterfalls and gaze at all of the sunsets. It is too short to do it all, and that is why it is such a precious privilege to be able to do any of it.

In my younger days, when I was learning to fly, I had to practice takeoffs and landings. After one particularly rough landing, something on the order of a controlled crash, I commented ruefully to my instructor, "That was a terrible landing, wasn't it?" His reply contained the wisdom of the ages. "It's a good landing if you can walk away from it!"

God is not interested in the style of our landings. Onlookers may cluck and comment and roll their eyes. But not God. When we, like Zusya, stand before our Creator to render an accounting of our lives, God's concern will not be with our sins and shortcomings. They are foregone conclusions. They are part of the admission fee that goes with risking the great adventure. No, God's concern will be with our ability to walk away from the landing with a sense of gratitude and amazement for having been given the opportunity to live.

11

Waiting in Hope

Waiting for Christmas to roll around is not easy. We become impatient—even frustrated—counting the days, or years, until the new creation matures. We wait for those new beginnings that have been promised; wait for the new life, the new being which is to be conceived in our flawed humanity and born as a child of grace within us. "It is, after all, only a story," we remind ourselves, and sometimes the evidence for trusting it is scanty at best.

But as believers, we have no real alternative. So we wait! Wait for the promise to be fulfilled. Hopefully, with kindled faith and in eager anticipation of the birth of the new within us. But, in any case, we wait.

For most of us, waiting is regarded as a necessary evil. The fact that sometimes it is necessary to wait does not diminish our regard for it as an evil, or at least, undesirable. To wait in a long check-out line at the grocery store is irritating. To be stopped on the way home by a changing traffic light and then delayed until it turns green is annoying. To wait for a plane that is late in arriving is a waste of time.

Most of us are accustomed to filling our time with activities. We set schedules and measure ourselves against them so that we can know how much progress is being made. We make lists of things to be done and check off the items as each is accomplished. Indeed, our identity or sense of worth is often tied to our accomplishments. Waiting is consciously or unconsciously felt to be a threat to our self-esteem. We have no patience with any apparent lack of progress in ourselves or in our society. Not to feel that "day by day in every way we are becoming better and better" is a vexing, if not depressing, realization.

When life finds us in such a place, stalled out in the mood of "those days," we can identify with the frustration of the psalmist. It may be scant comfort, but we have a lot of company! Impatient with God's delay, the psalmist can only wait . . . and hope for the promise to be kept.

> Out of the depths I cry to thee, O LORD!
>> LORD, hear my voice!
> Let thy ears be attentive
>> to the voice of my supplications! . . .
> I wait for the LORD, my soul waits,
>> and in his word I hope;
> my soul waits for the LORD
>> more than watchmen for the morning,
>> more than watchmen for the morning.
> (Psalm 130:1, 2, 5, 6)

In this world of frustration and impatience, with its emphasis on producing character and commodities, the poet's words reverberate. God comes to those who wait!

It is surprising how often the Bible speaks of renewal coming to those who wait for the Lord. "They who wait for the LORD, shall renew their strength, they shall mount up with wings like eagles, they shall run and not be weary, they shall walk and not faint" (Isaiah 40:31). Or the psalmist again:

> I believe that I shall see the goodness of the LORD
>> in the land of the living!
> Wait for the LORD;
>> be strong, and let your heart take courage;
>> yea, wait for the LORD! (Psalm 27:13-14).

The apostle Paul contemplates the required wait of the whole universe: "I consider that the sufferings of this present time are not worth comparing with the glory that is to be revealed to us. For the creation waits with eager longing for the revealing of the sons of God" (Romans 8:18-19).

Even the Most High had to wait. We may wonder why Gabriel was not sent a hundred years sooner? Why so long a wait? What was so special about that time? Those days? The storytellers leave the speculations to our imagination. They simply say God had to wait for the "fullness of time" (e.g., Mark 1:15 and Ephesians

1:10). Even then, the Most High had to wait on the pregnancy of Mary. Nine long months had to be endured before God could bring the Word into the world.

Imagine the divine impatience as the little boy Jesus grew up one day at a time, maturing slowly into adulthood! First he had to learn to toddle and talk. The Word was burning to be spoken, but God had to wait. What an eternity that must have seemed for the Most High as the years slowly rolled by; waiting for Jesus to learn to talk, waiting while he gained the needed experience to speak the mature Word. Thirty more years the God of the Ages had to wait before the message was spoken. Those thirty years must have seemed as long to God as the preceding thirty centuries.

We may wonder why all this emphasis on *waiting* in the Bible. Is it simply because waiting is a normal part of life? It takes time to heal physical injuries and emotional wounds. A pregnancy cannot be hurried. Not even by God. It takes nine months, and all the impatience in the world—or in heaven—will not hurry the process along. It is a frustrated farmer who attends his scattered seed day and night, hoping that by coaxing it along it will sprout and grow more rapidly. Not until the time is fulfilled will it do so. Waiting is his only option. We could observe that life does not reveal its meaning in a flash of insight. It unfolds over a period of time: year by year, experience after experience. There is no hurrying the process. We have to wait. Is this why the Bible speaks of waiting? Because it is simply a normal part of life?

I think not. The focus on waiting called for by the Advent season in the church calendar as the slow roll of time brings us week by week, Sunday by Sunday, to Christmas—all of this serves as an important reminder that waiting is a necessary part of our relationship with God. Rather than something to be regarded as a waste of time or a tolerated evil, waiting is a normative part of the life of faith. Emmanuel comes to those who are willing to wait.

We may ask why is this so? What is the hidden wisdom in waiting?

Any attempt at an answer may be presumptuous, but we know from experience that waiting makes it abundantly clear we are not in control of the circumstances. Waiting is the vocation of the powerless. In our power-conscious culture, where being in charge is crucial to our identity and self-esteem, waiting forces us to face the fact that we are not God. It serves as a reminder, as indeed we occasionally need reminding, that we are only human beings. Created in the image of God, yes! But that is not the same as being God. There is a difference between God and humanity. Paul Tillich summarizes the difference and the dangers in forgetting them.

> The condition of man's relation to God is first of all one of *not* having, of *not* seeing, *not* knowing, and *not* grasping. A religion in which that is forgotten, no matter how ecstatic or active or reasonable, replaces God by its own creation of an image of God. Our religious life is characterized more by that kind of creation than anything else. I think of the theologian who does not wait for God, because he possesses Him, enclosed within a doctrine. I think of the Biblical student who does not wait for God, because he possesses Him, enclosed in a book. I think of the churchman who does not wait for God, because he possesses Him, enclosed in an institution. I think of the believer who does not wait for God, because he possesses Him, enclosed within his own experience.[18]

Waiting reminds us of our limitations, of the basic fact of human existence: We need God. The human equation is not complete without the divine factor. We are not the center of the universe, nor is the Holy One at our beck and call. Being forced to wait underscores the fact that the power to deliver us from our predicament is not ours to command.

That is why biblical Israel knew so much about waiting. In the opinion of the world, she was a third-rate power. In her saner moments she had no illusions about her ability to change the course of history nor hope of escaping her predicament as a pawn in the affairs of larger, more powerful nations. Israel knew that control of her destiny did not rest in her hands. Therefore she looked forward to, and waited for, the coming salvation of the Lord.

By contrast, we can see why it is so difficult for us as Americans to wait. We suffer from a Messiah complex in which we assume that by our might we will bring peace and prosperity to the world. By flexing our military muscles we think we can enforce our will on others and with our technological prowess solve the problems of the world. We carry this love affair with our capabilities right into our churches, where it is nourished by countless sermons which suggest that, by flexing our motivational muscles and gritting our teeth, we can change ourselves and overcome our flaws. Perhaps we are disappointed with our slowness of heart. Filled with doubts, we find our faith a wooden thing, lifeless. Perhaps we are discouraged by our apparent lack of progress in overcoming some stubborn trait within ourselves that we can no longer tolerate. Or perhaps we are just plain tired of fighting some compulsion and feel that we are not winning the battle; we seem to take one step forward and two backward. Well-meaning religious cheerleaders urge us on from the sidelines. "You can be a beautiful person, if you try. Work at it! Think positively!"

The problem with such assumptions is that the more sincere we are about doing something to make ourselves acceptable in our own eyes as well as God's, the more frustrating the struggle becomes. Paul's cry speaks for all of us: "I do not understand my own actions. For I do not do what I want, but I do the very thing I hate. . . . I can will what is right, but I cannot do it. For I do not do the good I want, but the evil I do not want is what I do" (Romans 7:15,18-19).

When we have been overwhelmed by that kind of frustration, and engulfed by the dark night of the soul, we stand with waiting shepherds on the cold hills overlooking Bethlehem. We know that the power to change ourselves does not lie at our disposal. We can only long for the day of deliverance and the joy that cometh in the morning. Until then, we have starlight to live by and the psalmist's testimony, which offers us a word of encouragement. The salvation of God comes to those who wait.

Paul's experience led him to the same conclusion. "Thanks be to *God,* who gives us the victory" (1 Corinthians 15: 57). The good news is that the Holy One has the power even if we do not. Waiting reminds us that we are not God and cannot push the stream. But waiting also reminds us that there is One who brings deliverance in the fullness of time. The birth of Jesus is the guarantee of God's faithfulness.

Note, this kind of waiting is not inactivity. It is not to be confused with laziness. Waiting is an *activity of faith.* Waiting for God's deliverance is disciplined believing. It is living as though. . . . As though God's power is at work in our lives even though we may not be aware of it nor see any immediate evidence to support the claim. Instead of doing nothing, waiting means living actively as though we believe that the salvation of God is coming to us. Just as the conception of Jesus lies beyond human explanation, so the growth of the new being in us lies beyond our capabilities. It rests securely in God's care and keeping. And because of this, its coming is assured.

And lest we forget that the child of grace has, in fact, been promised, listen to the storyteller, John, as he quotes Jesus:

> I will not leave you desolate; I will come to you. Yet a little while, and the world will see me no more, but you will see me; because I live, you will live also. In that day you will know that I am in my Father, and you in me, and I in you (John 14:18-20).

When I was doing graduate work at the University of Edinburgh, James Stewart, professor of New Testament studies, was fond of saying, "Gentlemen and ladies, do you realize that one day we will stand in the presence of the angels? And they will gaze in wonder at us and say, 'My, how like Jesus they are!' "

To believe that God's continuing creative activity has come to the world in Jesus is to live as though the gestation is now at work within us, creating the new life, the new being that has been promised.

Nevertheless, even though the Christ has been conceived within us and his birth assured, there is still no way the pregnancy can be hurried along. We can only wait for the birth to come in due time. The waiting, therefore, needs to be filled with active preparation based upon disciplined believing that in nine months, that is, in the fullness of time, the birth will take place for all to see. Indeed, others may see it long before we are aware of it.

None of us was born suddenly. Birth came to us after having waited patiently in silence and darkness. When the anguished cry, "O wretched person that I am. Who will deliver me from this bondage to death?" has been wrenched from us and we have been forced to kneel mutely before our own inadequacies, waiting becomes the only option left to us. Just at the time when it seems as though nothing is happening, when we are discouraged and impatient, just at *that* time we need to read again the Christmas story and discipline ourselves to live as though new life is being created. Precisely when all of the evidence seems to point to the contrary and there is no reason on earth to assume that we will ever be any different—when it seems we are plagued by the same old temper and jealousy, troubled by the familiar feelings of inadequacy and inferiority—at that point we are to wait.

But we wait for God. And that is the good news, for our waiting is neither an activity of futility nor of passive acquiescence. We *actively* wait for God, assuming that the new creature is maturing in that silent, dark aloneness. Waiting is disciplined believing—believing the promise that the God of Abraham, Isaac, and Jacob, not to mention Sarah, Rebekah, and Rachel, and the God of our Lord Jesus Christ will keep the promise made and is, in fact, creating in us at this very moment the new creature that is worthy of being called "Child of the Most High."

The Old Testament reveals a long history of expectation, making it clear that the Christ was awaited a long time before his advent. Therefore, we must be prepared to wait another long time for his coming. But the message of hope is spoken to those who wait, actively believing that the promise will be kept. We have been assured that we do not wait in vain.

When it comes, the advent of the new being always catches us by surprise. Tillich counsels,

> Nothing is more surprising than the rise of the new within ourselves. We do not foresee or observe its growth. We do not try to produce it by the strength of our will, by the power of our emotion, or by the clarity of our intellect. On the contrary, we feel that by trying to produce it we prevent its coming. By trying, we would produce the old in the power of the old, but not the new in the power of the new. The new being is being born in us, just when we least believe in it. It appears in remote corners of our souls which we have neglected for a long time. It opens up deep levels of our personality which had been shut out by old decisions and old exclusions. It shows a way where there was no way before.[19]

That "way" does not lie in the present reality, but always in the future. Waiting directs our attention to the future wherein our hope resides. The storytellers of the Bible almost always include a future tense when speaking of the saving power of God. Old Testament prophets refer to the coming day of the Lord when God will redeem the people. New Testament writers see that day having arrived in Jesus' birth and life, but even when they speak of it, they always include a future tense and speak of his second coming.

To wait, therefore, is to affirm that this present situation, this present condition, no matter how good or bad, is *not* the kingdom of God. Waiting presupposes that something is yet to happen, that the present is not the end of the adventure, that there is something yet to be hoped for and lived toward. "It's not over," as the unrefined opera patron declared, "until the fat lady sings." Or in this instance, it is not over until the angels sing. Waiting invites us to live on tiptoes because the best view of the scene lies just over the horizon. Not only is more to come, but the best is yet to be.

People who change society and make a difference in the way things are, are people who can wait. Visionaries who cannot wait are little more than social gadflies who come and go with the changing fashions and the latest fads. This may be another reason why the Bible is so concerned about cultivating the ability to wait.

The activists of the 1960s crowded college campuses across the country. They were occupied with dreams of changing the world, creating a new society, righting the wrongs of the disenfranchised, and redressing the grievances of the poor. But the world had gone about its entrenched ways for a long time, and society proved to be a stubborn resister to change. Neither yielded readily to the advocates of the new order. The wrongs were not redressed; the grievances were not corrected. As a result, many of the student activists of the 60s at first became impatient, then cynical, and finally self-centered, as they returned to their campuses to throw frisbees, look inward through meditation, and graduate intent on making money. They could not wait.

Biblical faith, on the other hand, has sustained a social revolution for nearly two thousand years because it has cultivated patience: the ability to wait. The Old Testament prophet Habakkuk speaks of this patient pressure in a time of despair among his own people.

For still the vision awaits its time;
　　it hastens to the end—it will not lie.
If it seem slow, wait for it;
　　it will surely come, it will not delay (Habakkuk 2:3).

Israel's hope as a nation fed on such a faith story. Her citizens literally bet their lives on its assumptions. Habakkuk's words are as appropriate for our day as they were for his.

People who can wait live in the present but have their eyes glued to the horizon. They lean in the direction of time's flow. They live as though . . . the future is where the fulfillment of their waiting is to be found. Their minds do not wander. Their attention does not stray. And they do not become cynical. Their hopes are fixed on the new day and they wait, single-mindedly and expectantly, for the kingdom of God to come with its new creation. Nothing less will satisfy or fulfill them.

Waiting is a rehearsal for faith. By focusing our attention on the future, the practice of waiting trains us for dreaming and gives us the patience to actively await the fulfillment of those dreams rather than becoming impatient and frustrated. Waiting is another name for *hoping*—hoping for what has been envisioned by the grace of God and seen by the light of a star.

Waiting, therefore, is not a waste of time. It is a skill to be valued and developed by every believer. Those in the Old Testament practiced it while looking forward to the coming of the Christ. The New Testament calls for it as we take up our custodial responsibilities for planet Earth, even as we look for the fruits of his abiding presence in our own lives. Israel's experience, as she looked forward to the coming of the Messiah, and the church's experience, as it looks to his return, help us see that waiting is a necessary part of our relationship with God and a normative part of our faith. It is for us a time of disciplined believing, when we prepare for what is assumed and hope for what is yet to be.

12

Back to Work

And suddenly there was with the angel a multitude of the heavenly host praising God and saying, "Glory to God in the highest. . . . " When the angels went away from them into heaven, the shepherds said to one another, "Let us go over to Bethlehem and see this thing that has happened, which the Lord has made known to us." And they went with haste, and found Mary and Joseph, and the babe lying in a manger. And when they saw it they made known the saying which had been told them concerning this child; and all who heard it wondered at what the shepherds told them. . . . And the shepherds returned, glorifying and praising God for all they had heard and seen, as it had been told them (Luke 2:13-20).

Whatever else the shepherds experienced in their encounter with the angelic host, it was certainly what psychologist Abraham Maslow calls a "peak experience." It was an experience their family and friends continued to talk about until the day when Johannes Gutenberg, a distant relative by marriage, invented the printing press and it could be passed on to us in a paperback edition.

For most of us Luke's birth narrative, not to mention the other Gospel accounts, has significance only at Christmastime. And for most of us the celebration of Christmas comes only once a year. As a result, the glow of the season soon dissipates when the holidays are over. The warm cheer and the merriment of the season rapidly recede into the background, and the Christmas story, along with the decorations, is forgotten for another year. The needles drop from the trees, the creches are put away, and we go back to work, back to the competitive routine, back to the world of irritations, back to the memos, back to tax forms and to dishes left in the sink.

So while the peak experience about which Luke speaks and which the shepherds were privileged to share may lie beyond most of us, we can all identify with the frustration that their return to work must have occasioned. It was an abrupt change from the earth-shattering proclamation that the great Messianic age had arrived, back to jobs that by no stretch of the imagination would ever change the course of history. From the adoration of the Son of God to work that any fool could do. From the warmth of family love to drab fields, unyielding in the cold chill of the night. Back to the stark practicality of the next day.

Yet, while we can identify with the frustration of the shepherds, there is a difference. The shepherds, Luke claims, returned to work, ''glorifying and praising God.''

Why, we must wonder!

Were they happy to get back to work? Did they enjoy being shepherds so much that they could not wait to return to their sheep?

No one will ever convince me this was the case. Anyone who has ever worked with sheep knows that the critters are stupid, stubborn, and smelly. More than once the shepherds must have thought to themselves, if not out loud, ''There's gotta be a better way of making a living than this!''

Many of us find the responsibilities of work heavy and tiring. We can be grateful that Luke's telling of the story does not try to extol the greatness of work. Those who find work fulfilling do not need the Bible to proclaim its virtues. They know them already. But the fact is that many of us find work vexing and frustrating.

I suspect the feelings of my college roommate are not foreign to many workers. Upon awaking in the morning, he would sit on the edge of his bed, scratching, stare at the floor with glazed eyes and a dazed expression on his face, and moan, ''Oh Adam, what hast thou done?''

Work: A necessary evil forced on us by the shortsightedness of Adam or by practical necessity. And the fact that it is necessary does not alleviate in the slightest our dislike of it as an evil. Our attitude is something like, ''If it's all the same to you, I'd just as soon be somewhere else.'' Who has not come to the last day of the work week with the T.G.I.F. feeling? In case you have not, it means: Thank God, it's Friday! Even during the other six days, it is the rare exception when we wake in the morning with the words, ''Good morning, God,'' on our lips. More likely it is, ''Good God, it's morning!'' And if not cynicism, then quiet desperation.

How do we extol work as something significant and ennobling when many simply find their jobs neither? In a society of planned obsolescence, what is honorable about making or selling an appliance that you know has been designed to go out of style or break down in four of five years? The very term ''selling'' usually implies talking customers into purchasing a product for which they previously had neither need nor desire. The fingers of cynicism have fastened themselves around the neck of our working life.

Yet, the puritan work ethic has made us feel that we must work in order to justify our existence as human beings. We have to earn our worth. Consequently, when we are not working we feel guilty. We have long since lost the art of playing. Many of us have long ago buried the child within, in the frantic scramble to become adults. Play is not a useful skill in our competitive society. We work at our play. And our work has become compulsive. The joy is gone, if indeed it was ever there. Often the only reward in the drudgery is the paycheck that we receive, and it is almost never felt as adequate compensation. That, in itself, erodes the sense of self-worth because we feel we are selling our soul to the highest bidder. Work is not living. It is only a means to an end. We work in order to have the financial where-with-all to make true living possible.

It is precisely the fact that the shepherds were probably no more enthusiastic about going to work than we are that makes this story, and the difference in their return to it, so significant. They returned ''glorifying and praising God!''

The question is now all the more insistent: Why? Luke's narration is both interesting and revealing. He says, ''[They] returned, glorifying and praising God for all they had heard and seen.'' So, what was so great about what they had heard and seen?

Certainly it was not merely a cute little baby and his devoted parents standing by, a scene frequently portrayed by contemporary Christmas cards. The shepherds must have experienced more than the cozy joy of being invited to be a part of such a touching scene. Many of us have felt the being invited to be a part of such a touching scene. Many of us have felt the being invited to be a part of such a touching scene. Many of us have felt the warm glow of family love in our own lives, not to mention that of the holiday season. Yet, many of us still find our work vexing and frustrating. No! Whatever else the shepherds heard and saw, it had to have been something more significant than the charm of a baby, something that had the power to deliver them from the futility and frustration of having to go back to those stupid sheep.

Luke says they saw a Savior. The root meaning of the word *Savior* is "to deliver." The shepherds had seen in Jesus someone who was able to deliver them from the frustration of going back to work.

But in what sense was Jesus their Savior? It had to be something other than that offered by any traditional understanding of "Savior," such as one who could forgive sins. Forgiveness would not have sent them back rejoicing. As good Jewish shepherds they already had available to them the religious apparatus of the good Jewish sacrificial system which, in turn, made available to them God's forgiving love. As forgiven sinners they were still not excited about the prospect of working with those smelly sheep. Because a clear conscience had not been able to deliver them from their lack of enthusiasm for work, Jesus must have been a Savior in some deeper sense than merely one who came to forgive us our trespasses.

Nor could they have been delivered from the frustration of returning to work because they had been inspired by his great preaching and teaching. They had not heard Jesus tell them how splendid it was to be a shepherd, how noble it was to work with sheep, or how God could use their effort to benefit the whole of the human race. Later, Jesus would hold crowds spellbound, and his message would offer hope and inspiration to the multitudes; but all of that lay in the future. At this point in his budding career he could not yet talk. All that he could do was nurse at his mother's breast, babbling and blowing bubbles. Besides, if they had heard anyone try to convince them about the magnificence of being a shepherd, they might have returned to work with merriment, but not because they had met a Savior. More likely a fool! They would have laughed at the foolishness of anyone who could think that working with stubborn sheep was ennobling in any sense.

In what sense, then, was this baby a Savior?   He was a Savior to the shepherds precisely because he was born in a barn. It was his *style* of coming that made him a Savior. His style of coming had freed them from the necessity of apologizing for being shepherds with sheep dung on their sandals. It was the *modus operandi* of this Savior that delivered the shepherds from the compulsive need to justify their existence before God and the world. He had delivered them from the feeling that their work and everything else in their world, was somehow not quite respectable enough for the high and mighty of earth and heaven.

Jesus was their Savior because he was not born in a cathedral or in the sterile delivery room of a hospital. He was born in a barn. Not a clean new barn. Not even a redecorated barn. Jesus was Savior because he was born in a manure-ridden stable, to a couple whose relationship was not ideal. All of which made Jesus a Savior in the shepherd's eyes because he was not born in an ideal world of love, beauty, and perfection. Society had not freed itself from the tyranny of the establishments, either political or ecclesiastical, despite the protestations of its youth and its prophets. Jesus was a Savior because he was born in a world of Roman rule and oppression where people, in order to survive, had long since learned to compromise their integrity and rationalize it as necessary. Jesus was a Savior because he shared in the scandal of Bethlehem, in "those days."

Consequently, the shepherds went back to their quite menial work with no illusions about its grandeur nor its benefit to humankind. But they went back to work singing because they had seen a Savior in an unswept, very ordinary, and totally mundane barn. The sheep to which they were returning would be just as stupid, stubborn, and smelly as they had ever been. But the stupidity, stubbornness, and smell somehow no longer mattered. The shepherds' work would not alter the course of history one whit. But the fact that they would not leave a record of significance behind them was of no consequence now. The children waiting for them at home would be just as sassy as ever. But disrespect somehow was more tolerable. Family devotions would be missed more times than they would be observed at the evening meal.

But the guilt was now gone. They did not have to spruce up their world or put on clean underwear as if preparing for a papal visit. The Savior had already come. They did not have to get their act together in order to make room for God. The Savior had shown up on *their* turf. He had been born in their kind of world, with all of its imperfections and irritations, its vexing frustrations and compromises. The Savior was alive and well in a barn, and they had seen him.

And while the shepherds left behind no theological commentary such as the apostle Paul did, we can still imagine that as they went back across those dark, drab fields, reflecting on all that they had seen and heard, two things must surely have impressed them. First, that God had embraced life as it really was. God had shown them in this Savior—in his manner of coming—that the Most High had accepted the reality of sheep that should be smarter, but are not. The Holy One had affirmed a line of work that ought to be more noble, but is not. God had found satisfactory a couple who ought to have lived happily ever after, but did not. And parents who ought to be more patient with their children, but are not; not to mention children who ought to act more responsibly, but do not. "If this quite ordinary and almost totally irreverent life is good enough for God," the shepherds might have mused, "then it is good enough for us." No more need to make apologies for being shepherds, no more excuses for working with dumb, dirty animals. If this world was good enough for God, and if the Most High could put up with it, then it was good enough for them.

The second thing that might have caused the returning shepherds some giddiness was they had discovered God's sense of humor. Unlike tradition-bound churchgoers who have had their funny bones anesthetized by an overdose of solemnity and can no longer see anything remotely humorous about God or ecclesiastical operations, these humble shepherds, who probably had not darkened the doorway of a church for years, were still alive and alert to the comical side of things. They could respond, not only with songs of praise, but with laughter. Everyone had gone to the cathedral in Jerusalem for Christmas Eve services, and God had shown up in a barn at Bethlehem. It was as though God were saying, "Don't be surprised if I show up in your tent tonight. If a barn is not beneath me, certainly your tent is not out of bounds."

Suddenly everything became pregnant with the potential of divine disclosure.

The Gospel stories surrounding the life and death of Jesus are filled with God's grace-full sense of humor. By all odds, both Bethlehem and Calvary should be places that any sane person-would avoid. They are places undesirable, if not downright dangerous, to our health and happiness. But, as we have seen, we keep returning to them at Christmas and Easter with great joy and celebration because behind the stories of Bethlehem and Calvary lies the same grace-full experience: humor. Yes, humor!

Humor is that graceful view of life that refuses to take a given situation seriously. It does not look at things as they are and, therefore, will not allow the facts to define the reality. Humor looks at the predicament from a different perspective and sees another kind of reality: the reality of grace. By refusing to recognize the situation as Lord, it transcends the tragedy. Sometimes people who are frightened joke. The humor frees them from the incapacitating power of their fears. When people who are nervous laugh, the humor neutralizes the embarrassing power of self-consciousness. Humor is powerful.

Jesus Christ is the embodiment of God's powerful humor. The *modus operandi* of the Most High is not to eradicate scandal and death but to play "one-up-man-ship" with them. The Holy One tops their best line. God overpowers them with divine humor.

As God's sense-of-humor-made-flesh, Jesus, by his birth, death and resurrection, refuses to take our human limitations and liabilities seriously. God will not allow them to define us. Of course, if we read these stories without a sense of humor they become stone cold sober, and life is seen as deadly serious business. Their intention, however, is to free us from the deforming labels of "scandal" and the destructive powers of sin and death with "exceeding great joy," that is, laughter. Because they are seen from a different perspective, their stranglehold on us is broken.

A cartoon depicts two hapless fellows chained hand and foot, suspended by ropes over a pit filled with crocodiles. Sharpened swords protrude from the sides of the pit. The situation is quite hopeless. Nevertheless, one fellow says to the other, "Now, here's my plan."

Into the deadly serious human predicament, with all of its

apparent hopelessness, God delivers the divine Word with its punch line. Suddenly, all human limitations—neurotic jealousy and anger, self-consciousness and incapacitating pride, failure and scandal, weakness and death—all are viewed in a different light. Starlight! To us, caught in the despair of the predicament, the Comical One offers a Word of humor. The Word becomes flesh and we behold God's laughter. And for us the good news of great joy is that God has the last laugh. As Jesus hangs forlornly on his cross, God says, "Now, here's my plan." And the plan is Resurrection.

The best lines of death and despair are topped by God. God is the Top Banana! The Resurrection is God's sense of humor and it inverts our understanding of things.

Both Bethlehem and Calvary, and the stories surrounding them, remind us of the central miracle to which the New Testament bears witness. God is a Comedian who meets us in the midst of real life with all its seaminess and sadness and brings joy and laughter.

So, the shepherds returned glorifying and praising God because God had tickled their funny bone. What amused them was the way the Most High had bypassed the ecclesiastical bigwigs. God had shown them that the divine Word could be spoken quite eloquently without benefit of a priesthood—a priesthood that had come to assume God would be tongue-tied without them. Long before twentieth century theologian Karl Barth used such delightful images, the shepherds were dimly aware that God could speak through "Russian Communism, a flute concerto, or a dead dog." It was as though God had nudged them in the ribs that night in Bethlehem and said, "If you think this is good, wait till you see where I'm going to show up tomorrow."

Happily, the humor has not gone unnoticed by Matthew, though we who read his narrative frequently miss it. In his account, he offers us this cartoon. Picture wise men from the East making inquiries of the learned religious leaders: "Where is your long-expected king to be born? We know he has at last come for we have seen his star!" The scholars, knowledgeable in such matters, knew in just which books to look for the answer and so informed their visitors. "Bethlehem, for so it is written." But, while the wise men departed to worship the long-awaited Jewish Messiah, the learned Jewish leaders simply continued their reading. They had missed the whole point of their learned religious tomes, and the gospel train left without them.

One of the non-traditional Christmas carols catches Matthew's point when, in its own slightly ridiculing way, it proclaims, "Tell to Old Jerusalem that Christ is born in Bethlehem." Old Jerusalem was the respected and respectable religious establishment for the Jewish people. Old Jerusalem had all of the answers to all of the God questions. If God were to make a divine disclosure, it would certainly be there among the learned theologians, or so they assumed. Any Messianic figure worth his salt would have to receive his credentials from the religious authorities who were quartered in the capital. As far as the bureaucratic brass in Jerusalem were concerned, it was utterly unthinkable that the Messiah would check in without paying his respects at the ecclesiastical embassy. Certainly, news of an illegitimate child born in a Bethlehem barn could be of no interest to them.

The punch line, so far as the Gospel narratives are concerned, is that God was fully aware of this. It is their ironic assertion that the Holy One chose to disregard all of the niceties of religious protocol and showed up in Bethlehem. And even there, not in the VIP suite of a Ramada Inn, but in the garage out back. Those who could speak most authoritatively about the theological doctrine of the incarnation were not those professional theologians in Jerusalem with their seminary degrees, but infidels from the East and uneducated, and probably hopelessly irreverent, shepherds.

Maybe it is no big thing that the shepherds returned glorifying and praising God. But we live in the same kind of irreverent world, working at the same kind of uninspiring jobs: adding up figures, wiping runny noses, selling ships, shoes, and sealing wax. And it is the same Savior, whose birth we celebrate once a year, whose story reminds us all year long that God has accepted this very uninspiring and scandalous world and all of us who inhabit it. I lay it before you that if shepherds could return glorifying and praising God, so can we . . . if we, like them, remember what has been told us about a barn in Bethlehem, lighted by a star.

Epilogue:

"Tell Me a Story . . ."

It would be nice to have a big finish to the story, a climactic ending with the violins building to a crescendo and a camera fade-out. But this is the real world, not a Hollywood sound stage. Luke concludes his narrative simply, "the shepherds returned, glorifying and praising God for all they had heard and seen, *as it had been told them.*"

Perhaps it is enough, however, if we remember there was nothing about that baby born in a barn to distinguish it from a hundred other pathetic welfare cases except what had been *told* them by an angel. Let us also remember that, although we have never seen Jesus in the flesh as did the shepherds and wise men, we share a common bond with them. What binds us together is that we have all been *told* that the child is the Christ. The nativity narratives are to us what the angels were to the shepherds and the star was to the wise men. They point the way to Bethlehem where Emmanuel awaits us. Ours is a faith conceived and nourished by the Gospel stories, and those stories alone. Any benefits we have experienced in our lives because of that faith have been brought about by the power of the Jesus story as it has been told us.

We may wonder what is the power of his story: people picking up the broken pieces of their lives with a radiancy and a sense of buoyancy nothing short of miraculous. Empowered by the story of a star that shone over the landscape of their lives, they have been able to return to situations that would normally be thought of as overwhelming and desperate. They are able to go on as victors rather than victims. There is more than solar energy in this starlight. "I can do all things in him who strengthens me."

123

Paul said it first (Philippians 4:13), but legions after him have been able to repeat it with conviction.

The power is, I think, in the way the stories have been told, the way the narrations have been crafted as Gospel stories. Stories that deal with scandalous and mundane matters, yet have the power to create hope in the midst of despair, power to generate light that darkness cannot extinguish, power to nourish life in the face of death. Gospel stories!

Holocaust survivor Elie Wiesel, recalls his experiences in the death camps. He tells of one inmate, a madman, barely in touch with reality, who was part of the slave labor force:

> When he spoke, his lips barely moved and his voice seemed to come from a long way off. It was the voice of a man who challenges mountains.
>
> The place where I met him was dark, as though some magician had plunged it into eternal night; It was peopled with phantoms. There were countless thousands of them. They had no past and no future. They were outside of time, beyond history. They were building a one-way Jacob's ladder, gigantic and invisible, which they were all waiting to climb, so that the heavens might be purified by fire. Man was leaving the earth, recalled by God. Everything was to start again. Creation had failed. The age-old vision had degenerated into a curse.
>
> But my visionary friend refused to believe all that. He claimed that we were in the Holy of Holies, in the presence of the Messiah. What he lacked in humor, he made up in imagination. . . .
>
> We called him "the Prophet." . . . All I know is that [the name] suited him. The Prophet talked like a prophet. Making us relive our past, he gave us back our homes and our memories. And yet, as we listened in silence with lumps in our throats, it was always of the future that he spoke. The truth was that we needed a future.[20]

Wiesel, a Nobel laureate, chooses his words carefully to tell a tale of power and by so doing transforms an account of horror into a Gospel story. He sees his fellow inmate, not as a madman barely in touch with reality, but as a prophet who brings endurance to the exhausted, life to the living dead, and an identity to the nameless numbers. Wiesel recognizes in this bizarre figure a savior who brings a desperately needed gospel to the death camps.

Similarly, the accounts that the Gospel writers give us are every bit as significant as is the Christ who stands behind them. Our faith is indebted to them and their representation of Jesus as the Christ. For them to say that Jesus is not a madman, a fool, or a tragic hero is to present him for our consideration as a Savior. He is One who by his birth and lifestyle, his death and resurrection, stands before mountains and challenges them, challenges all of the assumed limits and labels, all of the traditional definitions that would assume "this is the way it is!" To see in Jesus a Savior is to see one who gives us a future, and we badly need a future.

Ironically, amazingly, humorously, providentially, Jesus is Savior because the beginning and ending of his story is cast in scandal. He was born in a barn. He was crucified as a criminal. We first see him by the light of a star, and our final look is through the blaze of the resurrection. He is illumined as the Christ.

The power of the Jesus story is the light of that star and the claim of his resurrection. We are invited to entertain the assumption that our Savior has overcome the guilt of living and the embarrassment of dying. We do not need to apologize for the warts, bumps, and scars that the risk of living as less than perfect creatures inevitably incurs. When we view the scandal of Jesus' life by the light of a star, we can see the flaws of our own humanity washed in the same starshine. Those stories, which we call "God's word," give us permission to rename our lives as precious gifts of divine grace.

But the story of Jesus not only calls us to live our lives with all their limitations and weaknesses. This, too, the stoic and cynic can do. Rather, this story gives us *permission to rename our limitations and weaknesses.* We are not locked into the names that have been assigned us, nor are the labels that have been pasted across our lives fixed.

The world looks at the life of Jesus with its questionable beginning and sees the cross as its bottom line. By the standards of the world we ought to conclude—when we are not caught up in a pious sentimentalism—that he died "prematurely"; his life began in "scandal" and ended in "failure." He was an "embarrassment" to his family and friends. To his disciples his ministry ended in "tragedy" and "disillusionment."

But the star and the resurrection are God's invitation to not only see things differently, but to rename them! The Holy One is saying, "You don't have to live with those labels. You are not confined to those categories."

The birth of Jesus aside, look at how believers have come to regard the crucifixion. The resurrection gives us permission to name the cross a symbol of "life," not death. It gives us permission to call it a symbol of "glory," not scandal. A symbol of "atonement," not a dead end. "New beginnings," not failure. It is a remarkable feat of faith that we dare to call the Friday of crucifixion, "Good Friday." The cross is not eradicated, but when we rename it, all of life's "failures" can be seen differently. John Gardner speaks of this inversion of grace as a series of great opportunities cleverly disguised as insoluble problems. Christian hope is not something we derive from the evidence. Christian hope is something we claim contrary to the evidence and only because the Most High gives us permission through a story to draw contrary conclusions, i.e. to rename the data. We have God's Word on it. That Word is "Jesus Christ," born in a barn, crucified on a cross, and raised to glory. His story gives us permission to rename our lives and our experiences *gracefully*.

One of the clichés of our culture is that love is blind, but marriage is an eye-opener. Not so! Love sees with amazing clarity—especially if it is God's love. Jesus' vision was a divine 20/20. He looked at a reckless Simon, but saw boldness. So he renamed him "Peter,". which means "rock." "And on this rock," Jesus said, "I will build my church" (Matthew 16:18).

Similarly, the Christ of the Gospels does not *change* us; he *renames* us. That is a crucial distinction. He does not do away with our neuroses. He simply renames them and calls them "gifts." Our idiosyncrasies, after all, are what make us interesting. They are what make us unique as individuals. Christ sees them as contributions to life. He does not remove our failures, he calls them "new beginnings." He does not wipe away our mistakes, he says that is how "wisdom" is fashioned. He does not deliver us from our handicaps, he calls them "challenges." And, most assuredly, he does not deliver us from our weaknesses, but rather calls them "strengths" to be shared.

Perhaps the most important gift that these writers give us in

126

their stories, which call us to a manger in Bethlehem and then send us on our way, is the star which goes before us lighting our path. The most important function of faith in Christ may not be that it saves souls and wins the door prize at the pearly gates— though it may do both—but that it gives us permission to rename our lives. And in so doing, we ourselves are, in some mysterious, even miraculous way, born anew.

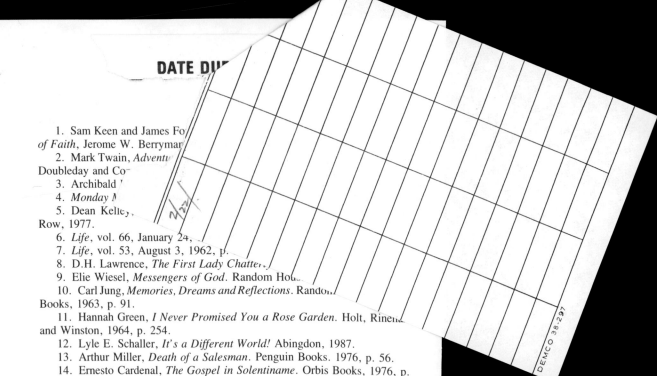

1. Sam Keen and James Fo⟨...⟩ *of Faith*, Jerome W. Berryman⟨...⟩

2. Mark Twain, *Adventu⟨...⟩* Doubleday and Co⟨...⟩

3. Archibald ⟨...⟩

4. *Monday* ⟨...⟩

5. Dean Kelley, ⟨...⟩ Row, 1977.

6. *Life*, vol. 66, January 24, ⟨...⟩

7. *Life*, vol. 53, August 3, 1962, p.⟨...⟩

8. D.H. Lawrence, *The First Lady Chatter⟨...⟩*

9. Elie Wiesel, *Messengers of God*. Random Hou⟨...⟩

10. Carl Jung, *Memories, Dreams and Reflections*. Random Books, 1963, p. 91.

11. Hannah Green, *I Never Promised You a Rose Garden*. Holt, Rinen⟨...⟩ and Winston, 1964, p. 254.

12. Lyle E. Schaller, *It's a Different World!* Abingdon, 1987.

13. Arthur Miller, *Death of a Salesman*. Penguin Books. 1976, p. 56.

14. Ernesto Cardenal, *The Gospel in Solentiname*. Orbis Books, 1976, p. 72.

15. Kurt J. Vonnegut, *Cat's Cradle*. Dell Books, 1963, p. 149.

16. Carl Jung, *Modern Man in Search of a Soul*. Harcourt, Brace, and World, 1933.

17. Lowell D. Streiker, *The Promise of Buber*. J.B. Lippincott, 1969, pp. 13-14.

18. Paul Tillich, *The Shaking of the Foundations*. Charles Scribner, 1948, pp. 149-150.

19. *Ibid.*, p. 182.

20. Elie Wiesel, *Legends of Our Time*. Holt, Rinehart and Winston, 1968, pp. 54-55.